AFRICAN MEXICANS AND THE DISCOURSE ON MODERN NATION

Marco Polo Hernández Cuevas

D1598827

University Press of America,® Inc.
Dallas · Lanham · Boulder · New York · Oxford

Copyright © 2004 by
University Press of America,® Inc.
4501 Forbes Boulevard
Suite 200
Lanham, Maryland 20706
UPA Acquisitions Department (301) 459-3366

PO Box 317
Oxford
OX2 9RU, UK

Library of Congress Control Number: 2004102476
ISBN 0-7618-2858-3 (paperback : alk. ppr.)

To the light:
Ignited by those who have been
Those who are and
Those who are to be

Contents

Foreword

I continue to be impressed with Dr. Hernandez's dedication and knowledge and the high quality work he has been able to turn out in such a short time. His contributions are unique and I enjoy his work very much. He writes well and the information he imparts is a revelation for the reader. His close reading of novels, for example, lays it all out in "black and white" in what are clearly original and eye-opening discussions. It is good that his work is now being published in book form.

Dr. Hernandez's book comes complete with a central organizing principle worth presenting and defending, which he does well. I am convinced his work will contribute greatly to the ongoing discussion of race in the Americas and particularly in Mexico where his research largely stands alone. The interdisciplinary approach he takes exemplifies the pervasive nature of the cult of whiteness and racism and their unfortunate byproducts in a nation that is far from white. Such countries as Mexico (and the Dominican Republic) need his kind of frankness to counter misrepresentation and denial, both historical and current. It is easy to be misled by José Vasconcelos and his pseudo science but Dr. Hernandez's work helps the reader get beyond that by pointing out the damage Vasconcelos has done in his time and in his legacy. He is certainly on the right track.

Dr. Hernandez's reading of *Pito Perez* (so interesting I was looking for a few more pages of discussion of it) and *La muerte de Artemio Cruz* are revolutionary as are the first two chapters of his book and the one on *Angelitos*. The material from the 1940s explosion onward he discusses is rich. Also, his chapters on film, the novel plus the two on culture and history all focus on the psychological effects of racism and the white aesthetic. All illustrate the pervasiveness of Vasconcelos' legacy in all genres covering all the periods under discussion, which Dr. Hernandez approaches chronologically right up to our time.

This is exciting good work as is the current research Dr. Hernandez has underway and there is still more to be done.

Richard L. Jackson

Preface

In *African Mexicans and The Discourse on Nation*, I explore how the Africaness of Mexican *mestizaje* was erased from the national memory and identity and how the national African ethnic contributions were plagiarized by the *criollo* elite in modern Mexico. I examine the discourse on nation in part of the salient narrative, film and popular culture forms that propagated the belief that only "white" was beautiful during a period I call "the cultural phase of the Mexican Revolution, 1920-1968." I look at the coding of "visibly" black Mexicans to unveil the connection between the black image distortion and the "vanishing" of Mexican Africaness, precisely when a national identity, that omitted its blackness, was forged.

I expose how the *criollo* elite, who saw themselves as white, and their lackeys who desire wholeheartedly to be considered white, disenfranchised the nation as a whole by institutionalizing a Eurocentric myth whereby Mexicans learned to negate part of their ethnic makeup. The credit to Africa for its overwhelming contributions to *mestizaje* was denied. In their Eurocentrically blinded determination to build a modern nation, through ideological homogenization, the self-proclaimed revolutionary government removed all blackness from the ideal Mexican image disseminated in and out of the country. This government was convinced that in order to take the country out of darkness and into the light, the population had to be whitened. During this epoch, and in the material studied, wherever African Mexicans— visibly black or not—are mentioned, they appear as "mestizos" oblivious of their African heritage and willingly undergoing whitening.

Acknowledgments

One day in the early eighties, I ran into a book that caught my attention while searching the library shelves at Portland State University: ***The Black Image in Latin American Literature*** by Richard L. Jackson. The title itself had a life-changing message for me. I took the book home and read it. There were many ideas beyond me, but I was able to grasp that while racism is outdated, its discourse and aesthetics are still being taught and practiced unchecked in the least expected places by the least expected people, at times unknowingly.

Dr. Jackson's work allowed me to think differently about myself. I became able to understand that *mestizaje* and *mulataje* in Mexico, as in other places of the Americas, are synonyms when viewed from the "*limpieza de sangre*" (or one-drop rule) perspective. Therefore, and for his further guidance and support in the making of this work, I remain indebted to Dr. Jackson. Also, I would like to take the opportunity to thank Dr. Kofi Agorsah, Dr. Derek Carr, Dr. Bill French, Dr. Marvin A. Lewis, Dr. Robert Miller, Dr. Gloria Nne Onyeoziri, Dr. Earl Rees, Dr. Ian Isidore Smart, Dr. Antonio Urrello, among other fine scholars and friends for their invaluable guidance, help, and support. Also, I wish to thank my family for their unremitting love and trust.

Introduction

For Edward Said, nations are narrations and the power of narrating and blocking the formation and emergence of other narratives "is very important for culture and imperialism, and it constitutes one of the most important connections among them" (Introduction, xiii).

According to Jose Piedra, Nebrija argued in 1492 "that language becomes the source of power when it provides an official 'home' for the memory of all who contribute to the empire, and grammarians act as the official guardians of such a home" (306).

Mestizos, or people of mixed blood constitute the largest percentage of the total population in Mexico.[1]   It is generally reported that mestizos represent anywhere from 55 to 85 percent of Mexican people. The common belief, even at present, is that this group or "minority" is the result of the exclusive mix of Amerindians and Spaniards. This partial truth was disseminated in Mexico, and outside the country, during a period herein identified as "the cultural phase of the Mexican Revolution (1920-1968)."

Today's Mexican mestizos, known throughout the colonial period (1521-1821) as *mezclas* or *castas*, began to be born shortly after the Spanish invasion in 1521. Yet to be acknowledged is the fact that these *mezclas* were the daughters and sons of an array of mixes that occurred among the vanquished Amerindians, the enslaved black Africans, the invading Spaniards, and other people, such as Asians.

The origin of the semantic problem may be explained further by the fact that during the colonial period the classification "mestizo" referred only to the offspring of Spaniard and Amerindian. However, it must be stressed that this was merely one classification among over a dozen and a half "racial" classifications of which the majority, at times obviously and at times imperceptibly, contained the black African element.

In 1946, Gonzalo Aguirre Beltrán added another dimension to the problem when he "rediscovered" a "black" population in Mexico's south Pacific Coast. He classified mestizos as Indo-mestizos, Euro-mestizos and Afro-mestizos based on appearance. As a result, the term "Afro-Mexican" seems to have become a synonym for the "visibly black" portion of Mexican mestizos in a growing body of academic work. The problem with this perception is that it creates an artificial division of Mexican mestizos based on the way people look. For instance, the black or African root of Mexican *mestizaje* has been referred to as the "Third Root." This, in the case of visibly black Mexicans, appears erroneous. In some instances it seems more appropriate to call the African element the first root, in others, the second, or the third, or fourth. It should be clear, particularly in the light of new readings of history,[2] that a considerable part of Mexican mestizos, even many whose appearance would make one believe otherwise, possess black African genes.

The majority of Mexican mestizos are descendants of the hundreds of thousands of black African enslaved people[3] that started to be brought to Mexico from the onset of Hernán Cortés' invasion. On the one hand, this understanding is crucial to dispel the myth that Mexican mestizos are the offspring exclusively of Amerindians and Spaniards. On the other hand, it is important as it helps clarify that when visibly black Mexicans are referred to, it is not a reference to a separate group: it is a reference to a portion of Mexicans that due to their looks alone were singled out by the racist *criollo* thought that controlled the discourse on nation during the cultural phase of the Revolution.

This work analyzes the coding and distortion of the image of visibly black Mexicans in and through literature, and film; and the omission of the African heritage in popular culture images or sites that, by way of official intervention became symbols, icons or credentials of national identity. It explores how the Africaness of Mexican *mestizaje* was erased from the collective memory and national imaginary and the

African ethnic contributions plagiarized in modern Mexico. This study examines part of the discourse on nation expressed in various cultural texts produced by authors who subscribed to the belief that only white was beautiful, between 1920 and 1968.

The premise of this work is that through the government, the *criollo* elite and their allies disenfranchised Mexicans as a whole by institutionalizing a magic mirror—materialized in the narrative of nation—where mestizos perceive a partial reflection of themselves. The Africaness of Mexican *mestizaje* was removed from the ideal image of Mexicaness disseminated in and out of the country. During this period, and in the material selected for study, wherever African Mexicans—visibly black or not—are mentioned, they appear as "mestizos" oblivious of their African heritage and willingly moving toward becoming white.

The critical foundation of this research rests mainly on two essays: "Black Phobia and the White Aesthetic in Spanish American Literature" by Richard L. Jackson; and "Mass Visual Productions" in *White Screens Black Images: The Dark Side of Hollywood,* by James Snead.

In "Black Phobia...," Jackson points out that defining "superior and inferior as well as the concept of beauty" according to how white a person is perceived to be is a "tradition dramatized in Hispanic literature from Lope de Rueda's *Eufemia* (1576) to the present" (467). Under the white aesthetic explained by Jackson, morality, civility, gallantry, bravery, prowess, industriousness, restraint, sincerity, intellectuality, good-heartedness, and love-for-life, among other virtues, are measured according to how white a person appears to be; in short, virtuosity is defined by whiteness.

For Snead, "the coding of blacks in film, as in the wider society, involves a history of images and signs associating black skin color with servile behavior and marginal status." Snead points out, "while these depictions may have reflected prior economic oppression of blacks, they also tend to perpetuate it." He clarifies that, "through the exact repetition which is film's main virtue, these associations became part of film's typological vocabulary..." (142). James Snead's perspective on "coding" adds another dimension to Jackson's readings under the "white aesthetic."

The coding identified by Snead uses three particular tactics, among others, to forge and perpetuate black stereotypes: "mythification," "marking," and "omission" (143). The tactic of mythifying whites as "powerful" and "civilized" ensures that blacks appear as meek and uncivilized. Marking, as applying paint to make blackness stand out, is done to highlight the color line. The omission of prominent black figures reproduces and perpetuates the myth that blacks are subservient. For Snead "codes are not singular portrayals of one thing or another, but larger, complex relationships" (142).

The following cultural texts are the focus of this work: the book-length essay, *La raza cósmica: misión de la raza iberoamericana* (*The Cosmic Race: Mission of the Iberian-American Race*)[4] (1925) by José Vasconcelos; a sample of ideal Mexican mestizo images that, once detached from their African component, were implanted in the collective memory and psyche through various means of mass persuasion; the picaresque novel, *La vida inútil de Pito Pérez* (*The Futile Life of Pito Perez*)[5] (1938) by José Rubén Romero; the film, *Angelitos Negros* (*Little Black Angels*) (1948) by Joselito Rodríguez; and the postmodern novel, *La muerte de Artemio Cruz* (*The Death of Artemio Cruz*) (1962) by Carlos Fuentes.

The texts mentioned above are examined to disclose how visibly black Mexicans are coded in accordance to a white aesthetic.[6] The corpus studied is confined to the cultural phase of the Mexican Revolution, 1920 to 1968. However, this study refers to other historical periods as deemed necessary to provide support and a context to analyze the contents of the works from a perspective herein called the African-Hispanic American approach, a critical view that reads texts concerning the black experience from a black perspective.

Chapter One, "The Revolution and Invisibility: African Mexicans and the Ideology of *Mestiz*aje in *La raza cósmica*," reveals the racist agenda forming the core of José Vasconcelos' "cosmic race" ideology. It exposes how, as soon as Vasconcelos was named Minister of Education in 1921, his perspective, which promoted physical and mental whitening of the population, began to be disseminated via major channels of mass persuasion such as public education, newspapers, radio, mural paintings, cinema, impressions of popular nationalism, and literature, among other media. This chapter uncovers how the African elements of Mexican *mestizaje* were systematically excluded paradoxically by integration. It exposes how at the time, under a perspective marked by black phobia and white aesthetics, it was argued that all non-whites were on their way to becoming some new shade of "white" due to natural selection and love.

The second chapter, "The Erased Africaness of Mexican Icons," examines the recasting process undergone by some of the most popular images and cultural expressions of national identity. It uncovers how, through this officially supported procedure, the Africaness, intrinsic to the development of said images and cultural expressions, was removed or diluted to disappearance. This chapter focuses on the manner in which these images and expressions, once "cleansed" from any reference to their blackness, were widely publicized and how after 1920 became icons of national identity.

"*La vida inútil de Pito Pérez*: Tracking the African Contribution to the Mexican Picaresque Sense of Humor," Chapter Three, analyzes the Mexican landmark picaresque novel, *La vida inútil de Pito Pérez*. It establishes a link between the first profane dances and songs of indisputable black roots and the popular Mexican satire, with *La vida inútil* and the sense of humor represented therein. It shows how the main character, Pito Pérez, essentially echoes Manuel Payno's characterization of the *mezclas*. These *mezclas*, which roamed the countryside and cities in very large numbers, were also known as "*léperos*," "*pelados*", or "*pícaros*," among other names. The chapter highlights the connection between *pícaros*, the Mexican sense of humor, and the *mezclas*.

Chapter Four, "*Angelitos negros,* a Film from the 'Golden Age' of Mexican Cinema: Coding Visibly Black Mestizos By and Through a Far-reaching Medium," discloses how international black stereotypes are used to code black Mexicans in and through film. It documents that cinematography was utilized along with literature and other channels of mass persuasion as part of a nationalist campaign to defame blacks while promoting whitening. This chapter exposes the racist discourse that went above and beyond cultural and linguistic barriers. It establishes a link between Hollywood's views and official Mexican views guided by black phobia and the white aesthetic in or around 1949, a time when *Angelitos* and other Mexican films such as *La negra Angustias* were made in Mexico.

The notion that the novel, *La muerte de Artemio Cruz* is a "new" way of telling the same stereotypical stories about blacks and their descendants is presented in Chapter Five, "Modern National Discourse and *La muerte de Artemio Cruz*: The Illusory "Death" of African Mexican Lineage." This part shows how through new structural technology, the reader is penetrated to the unconscious where, through the reinforcement of preexisting symbols, the author forges his negative images of blacks and their sons and daughters.

The objective of this study is to shed light on the manner in which the black African characteristics and the African legacy are narrated to disappearance or insignificance while coded under a white supremacy perspective in the following manners: by distorting or deliberately ignoring their beauty, their inner-strength and their world-views; and by misappropriating the African cultural contribution to Mexican *mestizaje*, a legacy imbedded in popular expressions such as dance, song, food and language.

In the works analyzed, black images are systematically portrayed within a process of assimilation through characteristics such as "green eyes" or other white features. For black characters to be rebellious or to show intelligence, they have to be diluted, deliberately ignoring that blacks from the onset of slavery began to revolt and that if they survived until the present in Mexico, as well as in other parts of the "New World," it was not due to miscegenation with "whites" but in spite of it and due to their own intelligence and inner strength. Even where an author appears to recognize the Africaness of a character, the analysis finds a narrative that distorts the image of African Mexicans by bleaching them out.

This same ideology, based on the white aesthetic, was instrumental in plagiarizing the African legacy to Mexicaness where it ascribed Spanish and Amerindian origins alone to various African Mexican cultural expressions that became icons of modern national identity. This analysis reads the works studied as part of the relationship between the ideology of *mestizaje* and the erasure of the Africaness of Mexican *mestizaje*.

Notes

[1] According to the official 2000 preliminary report from the XII census in Mexico the general population is 97,361,711 (INEGI).

[2] In *Historia General de México: versión 2000*, it is mentioned that to understand the confusion in terms, one must take into consideration the tendency to hide the origins of mixed blood since it was considered infamous (320, 321).

[3] It should be mentioned that many Spaniards carried black genes as documented in Chapter Two; and that some blacks landed with the Spaniards before the onset of the Transatlantic Slave Trade.

[4] All translations in this work are mine unless otherwise specified.

---

⁵ William O. Cord translated this title. See bibliography for full citation.

⁶ Jose Piedra traces through language the introduction and development of the white aesthetic in Latin America.

One

The Revolution and Invisibility: African Mexicans and the Ideology of *Mestizaje*[1] in *La raza cósmica*

> The African presence in Mexico
> as a whole has historically been
> minimized, if not ignored or even
> denied.
> Francis D. Althoff, Jr.

> [O]ne of the most interesting cases of
> the Negro in Latin America is
> the Negro that no longer exists.
> Richard Pattee[2]

> Homogenization as a civilizing act
> finds its greatest expression in José
> Vasconcelos' racism.
> Miguel Alberto Bartolomé

José Vasconcelos (1882-1959),[3] was the minister of education in Mexico from 1921 to 1924 at the start of the cultural phase of the Mexican Revolution. His ideology on *mestizaje* has been studied from a historical perspective by Alan Knight in an essay titled "Racism, Revolution, and *Indigenismo*: Mexico, 1910-1940" (71-113). Knight identifies him as one in a string of eugenicists[4] found throughout Latin

America and Europe at the end of the nineteenth century through the beginning of the twentieth century when the newly independent Latin American states were trying to become nations. Knight believes that Vasconcelos' racism is "reverse discrimination"[5] and, like Carlos Monsiváis,[6] claims that Vasconcelos "shifted" to the "right" later on in life. The premise of this study is that Vasconcelos personified the right in the Mexico of his days. His views (which affected all socially non-white Mexicans—over 80% of the total population) were *criollo* views, a sort of white supremacist racism proudly described as *la cultura criolla* (*criollo* culture) by Samuel Ramos in 1963 (91-109). Miguel Alberto Bartolomé, in 1997, explained that "homogenization as a civilizing act finds its greatest expression in José Vasconcelos' racism." He states that for Vasconcelos, "the mestizo would be the 'cosmic race,'" a sort of synthesis of all known "races called to hold world supremacy in the future" and therefore the logically determined referent in the process of national construction (28: n. 7). The present chapter focuses on Vasconcelos' essay, *La raza cósmica: misión de la raza iberoamericana.*[7]

La raza, a book-length essay and travel memoirs, is a pillar in the foundation of modern Mexico's national identity. Vasconcelos' philosophy regarding "racial" [8] and cultural mixing, manifested in *La raza*, had as the central goal the homogenization of all ethnicities in post-Revolution Mexico under the ideology of *mestizaje*.[9] Miguel Alberto Bartolomé clarifies: "after the Revolution of 1910, when the repression of cultural plurality became more intense, despite the rhetorical exegesis about the indigenous past, it was assumed that cultural homogenization was a necessary condition for the configuration of a modern nation" (27). To this explanation should be added that Vasconcelos' plan to Hispanicize Mexico, beyond its cultural aspects, included a racist[10] agenda whereby African Mexicans[11] were portrayed as inferior and caricatured.

This chapter analyzes the ideology of *mestizaje* in *La raza* and its white aesthetics. While recognizing that *mestizaje* ideology injured all non-whites in Mexico, this part concentrates on how Vasconcelos' program affected the portion of African Mexicans who were considered black due to appearance. It analyzes particularly the manner in which Vasconcelos' discourse was used as a foundation of an ideology that, from the start of the cultural phase of the Mexican Revolution, in 1920, made "visibly" black African Mexicans officially invisible at least until the mid 40s and that until today has blurred *mestizaje*'s Africaness and all African ethnic contributions to Mexicaness.

The African Hispanic American critical approach followed in this study is first introduced. Second, a brief historical account is given as background, starting with the Transatlantic Slave Trade, then the reader is placed at the time immediately after the armed phase of the Mexican Revolution when Vasconcelos enters the picture. Thereafter, Vasconcelos' beliefs are examined through the lens of Jackson's "black phobia and white aesthetics," paying close attention to the first 40 pages of *La raza* where Vasconcelos exposes his "doctrine for social and biological formation" (35).

It is established that in spite of a supposed total disappearance through absorption of *mestizaje*'s African characteristics (Sepúlveda 101; Garrido 1, 60),[12] in contemporary Mexico there are a number of Mexican communities, in more than one state, where Mexican Africaness is manifest.[13] It is also shown that, due to the power of Vasconcelos' illusion, Mexico's Africaness, at least in its irrefutable part, was not acknowledged until the mid forties when Gonzalo Aguirre Beltrán, an ethnologist and historian, carried out the first academically recognized fieldwork in communities of Guerrero state on the South Pacific coast of Mexico.

This chapter deals with the "racial" aspects of *mestizaje*. It exhibits *mestizaje* as an ideology that, while frequently understood as a breakaway move from the Eurocentric worldview, in fact perpetuated racism under a different guise.

As in the rest of the work, this chapter incorporates Richard L. Jackson's perspective whereby he explains:

Following a tradition dramatized in Hispanic Literature from Lope de Rueda's *Eufemia* (1576) to the present, the heritage of white racial consciousness, in Spanish America, as in Brazil and the non-Iberian countries, defines superior and inferior as well as the concept of beauty in terms of light and dark, that is, on the strength of the amount of whiteness one has. ("Black Phobia..." 467)

It is also argued that Jackson's views on the ideology of *mestizaje* stand acceptable. For Jackson, Vasconcelos' *mestizaje* type or "negative *mestizaje*" is "the process of restoring whiteness by bleaching out black people," a method called "ethnic lynching" that "has long been accepted in Latin America as a means of solving social and racial problems." A solution, as he points out, based on "the expectation that the biological superiority of the white race, augmented in number through European immigration, would impose itself on the non-white races" (*The Black* 3). Jackson also stresses: "the process of *mestizaje*, though of questionable value to the development of the black identity, is nevertheless, an indisputable fact of the black experience in Latin America" (*The Black* xv).

The Martinican psychiatrist, Frantz Fanon, in *Black Skin White Masks* (1952) presents an eye opening discussion of negative mestizaje, or whitening. In Brazil, Abdias do Nascimento treats the topic in, *O genocidio do negro brasileiro: proceso de un racismo mascarado* (*The Genocide of the Brazilian Black: The Process of a Masked Racism*) (1978). And the Costa Rican, Quince Duncan, in his "*Racismo: apuntes para una teoría general del racismo*" ("Racism: Notes for a General Theory on Racism"), exposes *mestizaje* as "*psicocidio racista*" (racist psychocide).   Duncan explains that by stigmatizing and diminishing everything related to black and indigenous populations, and by omitting their history and culture from the official history and culture "a process of ideological whitening is carried out by which the victim comes to feel disdain for herself and for everything that has to do with her and her race" (53).

Vera Kutzinski, in a reference by Edward J. Mullen, defines *mestizaje* as:

a peculiar form of multiculturalism, one that has circulated in the Caribbean and in Hispanic America, most notoriously in Brazil, as a series of discursive formations tied to nationalist interests and ideologies. This multiculturalism acknowledges, indeed celebrates, racial diversity while at the same time disavowing divisive social realities. (23)

Kutzinski's insight is of paramount importance in explaining Mexican post-revolution *indigenista* discourse—which includes African Mexicans under their mestizo hat—on ethnic relations, that casts the impression of a supposed ethnic harmony in Mexico. Ted Vincent elaborates:

Racial amnesia over African roots is common in Latin America, and usually can be traced to the master-slave relationship, which even after slavery is abolished leaves a belief among many dark complexioned Latin Americans that a successful life is one in which the children are lighter hued. Mexico puts an unusual twist on the Latin drift towards being white. In Mexico it is O.K. to stop at brown on the way to becoming white. Mexico calls itself "the cosmic race."   (2)

What is the Transatlantic Slave Trade and what is its relationship to the problem to be discussed here? Until 1873 black people, principally young women and men, were abducted out of Africa, under threat of deadly force, to be used as slaves for sex and work in Japan, China, Indonesia, Tasmania, India, Arabia, Europe and the Americas. In the nineteenth century, Africans also were among "the convict labor Britain sent to Australia from England, the West Indies, Mauritius and South Africa" (Harris 9).

The black African enslaved people taken to New Spain, today's Mexico, arrived mainly through the port of Veracruz. From there, they were taken all over the colony. The exact number of enslaved people taken to New Spain "legally" and illegally is unknown. What is known is that their presence became noticeable by the third quarter of the sixteenth century and that by the time of the War of Independence (1819-1821) black African blood, in different proportions, ran in the veins of Mexican mestizos. Mestizos until then had been classified into more than a dozen "racial" mixes known as *castas*[14] or *mezclas*. As much as 80% of these groupings refers to "racial" mixes where black African genes are present. It is also known that in New Spain, as in other European occupied places of the Americas, many of the enslaved Africans ran away and formed villages in hard-to-reach places starting in the sixteenth century. These rebels were called Maroons and their sagas became part of a narrative yet to be explored.

Slavery was banned in 1829 as the Mexican nation was budding. The large number of African descent *castas*, and the cheap labor they represented, made the import and keep of slaves unprofitable. The young nation was up for grabs and undergoing a series of internal struggles for power. At this juncture the idea of *mestizaje* emerged. The *criollo* led government was searching for a formula, an idea that would serve as cohesion for a deeply fractured population. According to Agustín Basave Benítez, the idea of *mestizaje*, in the beginning, ascribed the lack of order and anarchy to the "racial" varieties found in the population and therefore sought to eradicate them. The idea of *mestizaje* became then "a long-lived nationalist intellectual movement that presented *mestizaje* as the quintessence of Mexicaness" (15).

Basave cites José María Luis Mora, priest, politician and author of *México y sus revoluciones* (*Mexico and its Revolutions*), as expressing in 1849, "The need not only to end the uprisings of the *castas*, but to make it impossible thereafter, and the only way to achieve this is by the fusion of all races and colors present in the Republic into one" (Basave 24). The idea of *mestizaje* continued to grow under the shadows of other Eurocentric ideologies in the nineteenth century, such as liberalism, and it was not until after 1920 that it was officially instituted during Álvaro Obregón's government.

After ridding himself of Venustiano Carranza (1859-1920), Álvaro Obregón (1880-1928) became president of Mexico on November 30, 1920, as the armed phase of the Mexican Revolution dwindled. Obregón selected José Vasconcelos as his minister of education (Ramérez 217).[15] This appointment had dire consequences for the socially non-white, which reverberate throughout Mexico to this day. Amerindians and African Mexicans, who were mestizos of all shades and represented the majority of the Mexican population, with their languages, and cultural complexities, from the birth of modern Mexico, were cut off by Vasconcelos' vision of a super "race."[16]

Towards the end of the armed phase of the Revolution, around 1920, small armies, each led by a *caudillo*, were engaged in an all out war. This further divided a State that had been trying to emerge as a nation since the War of Independence against Spain (1810-1821). Tired of divisionism and fighting, people embraced at face value Vasconcelos' program of one "Latin-American" Mexico for all. What Mexicans ignored was that Vasconcelos' education program: was imposing the European Spanish language upon all;[17] and sowing his views on "race" while obscuring the true ethnic make-up of most of the fourteen million people who survived the Revolution.[18] Although *mestizaje* ideology had been in the making for some time in Mexico,[19] Vasconcelos is a key figure. He put theory into practice encouraged by those in power.

Hugh Thomas mentions: "In Mexico over 6,000 schools were built by the villagers themselves, without cost, by men on holiday, according to the ideas of a 'missionary' turned architect. Annex facilities in the shape of shower baths, sports fields, kitchens, among others, were sometimes added" (702 n. 32).   Gabriela Mistral recounts that Vasconcelos was given great resources to "civilize Mexico" and that "for the first time in the history of [Latin American] countries an education budget surpassed the United States education budget" (Bar-Lewaw 38). Paradoxically, even Mistral believed that for the first time American gold was being used for the superior interests of a people (Bar-Lewaw 39).

But what were the majority of Mexicans saying about a government program of "education" used to assimilate them into a culture that in fact excluded their ethnicities? After three hundred years of colonial rule, where education for the vanquished did not exist, and another one hundred years of factional wars, illiteracy was widespread in 1920. Spanish was the language of the ruling class. The majority of Mexicans spoke: Spanish as a second language; Pidgin Spanish; or did not speak Spanish at all.

Compounding the problem, although some means of communication were established during the *Porfiriato* (1876-1910)[20], on the one hand, was the fact that Mexico's interior was still largely cut off from the urban centers. On the other hand, the small towns and villages were cut off from one another, thereby making it impossible to organize any meaningful opposition. Toward the end of the armed phase of the Revolution the population at large had no voice, and where spokespeople emerged, like Emiliano Zapata and Francisco Villa, they were silenced. In some cases, such as Venustiano Carranza and Alvaro Obregón, the spokespeople became the oppressors.

Regarding people's silence, Frantz Fanon, as cited by Komla F. Aggor, in another context applicable here explains: "persons of African heritage tend to dislike and be ashamed of their own race not because of any intrinsic inferiority complex but as the result of being made inferior" (503). This is relevant under the present historical revision allowing one to see that the majority of Mexicans by the 1900s were the descendants of black Africans in various *mezclas* or degrees.[21]

According to the *criollo* creed on "races," Amerindians were as well inferior. *Criollos* and their lackeys continued to make them and their descendants believe as such. That is, the African and Amerindian ethnicities of most Mexicans were, and continued to be, regarded as traits of inferiority. As a response, for the most part, Mexicans became taciturn and as inconspicuous as possible and in this manner, they cooperated by omission with Vasconcelos' program for uniting the nation through homogenization. Thus, the path to achieve the total denial of the African component in Mexico's true identity began (Vincent 1-9).[22]

In 1971 Aguirre Beltrán, looking retrospectively, declared in an updated prologue to his 1946, *La población negra de México* (*The Black Population of Mexico*):

> all one has to do is give a quick look at the literature of 1910 to 1940, the crucial years of the revolutionary movement, to notice the preponderance of social studies on the Indian and, consequently, the absence of any mentioning of blacks as a sector of the population that in one or another manner could have contributed in the formation of the Mexican nationality. (9)

The "racial" and cultural ideology disseminated under Obregón and Vasconcelos in the early 20s through the *Secretaría de Educación Pública* (Ministry of Public Education) and via other means of mass persuasion such as the use of missionary teachers, radio, cinematography, literature and art, made "minorities" of black African descent invisible[23] in Mexico.

Aguirre Beltrán found in the mid 40s:

> in all cases where *mestizaje* in Mexico is spoken of, the authors make exclusive reference to the mix of the white dominating population and the defeated American population. Nobody is careful to consider the part that belongs to blacks in the integration of a culture in Mexico. (9)

Nina S. Friedemann, referring to the process of making a people invisible in Colombia, applicable here, explains:

> The invisibility in sociocultural processes is a strategy that ignores the present, the history, and the rights, of ethnic minorities. Its exercise implies the use of stereotypes, understood as absurd reductions of the cultural complexity, which pejoratively blur the reality of the groups thus made victims. (138)

Worthy of mention is that in spite of Friedemann's perspective about the negative impact of the blurring of ethnic complexities, Aguirre Beltrán's outdated views of a supposed integration process of African Mexicans are still being taught in Mexican schools (Garrido: 1, 60).

In *La población negra* mentioned above, Aguirre Beltrán, 46 years after the publication of *La raza*, still not free from Vasconcelos' spell, and under the belief that the Africaness of Mexicans would bleach out to disappearance eventually, referred to this blurring as "integration." And although at the end of his complex explanation he concedes, "there are a few black nuclei," he considers "integration" as an ongoing "process" (277-280). Nevertheless, 28 years after Aguirre's revision, these black enclaves continue to flourish, although until very recently they have been excluded from the collective memory by first diluting their very existence and then by caricaturing or ridiculing their image thereafter.

Bobby Vaughn, based on the 1990 population census, reports: "29 largely Afro-Mexican communities" in Guerrero and Oaxaca alone with a total population of 66,381.[24] Also, in a recent article by Jesús

Ramírez Cuevas, Estela Ramírez, a representative from the Sierra Zapoteca sur, while describing the situation of the indigenous people to members of the *Ejército Zapatista de Liberación Nacional* (*EZLN*) (*Zapatista* Army for National Liberation) reports that "from three and a half million Oaxacans, half are Amerindians and blacks" (2).

Luz María Martínez Montiel, in "Mexico's Third Root," explains: "[a]lthough strongest in black enclaves like Costa Chica, the African presence pervades Mexican culture. In story and legend, music and dance, proverb and song, the legacy of Africa touches the life of every Mexican" (2). She emphasizes the difficulty of tracing any one tradition as purely African after "five hundred years of blending with traditions of Indians and Europeans," and points out:

Compounding the difficulty is the fact that the African elements in Mexico's culture are not acknowledged as they are in other countries of the Americas. In fact *"el mestizaje,"* the official ideology that defines Mexico's culture as a blend of European and Indigenous influences, completely ignores the contributions of the nation's third root. (2)

Carlos Monsiváis points out that Vasconcelos, under the belief that "to educate" was "to populate," sought "to incorporate into the nation the indigenous minorities through the national school system," because Vasconcelos thought that Amerindians were "Mexicans first and then Indians." Moreover, Monsiváis explains that Vasconcelos was convinced that, "the indigenous dialects [could] not be educational tools," that "they [should] be eliminated giving way to the Spanish language," and that "the Indians [would] have to make this last acknowledgement of the victory of the conquerors." According to Monsiváis, Vasconcelos opposed Manuel Gamio's plan for 'integral action' (where he had "broken the nation into ten Indian regions for betterment and educational special projects") under the argument that "the politics of educating the Indian...in accordance with separate norms of any kind, not only is absurd among us, but it would be fatal" (Notas 1419).

This must not be construed as implying that Manuel Gamio (1893-1960) was opposed to Vasconcelos. Although Gamio is one of the precursors of *indigenismo* (revaluing of Amerindians), and he encouraged Aguirre Beltrán to study African Mexicans, Bartolomé indicates that for Gamio:

> the idea of nationality pre-supposed the homogenization of cultures (he
> called it 'fusion') of the races and the linguistic unification of the State's
> inhabitants, this perspective guided the *indigenista* scholars for more than
> a half century in their fundamental task: to help in the construction of the
> nation. (27: n. 7)

According to Castro Gómez, "the reduction of all cultural differences
to one principle—a *mestizismo* or romanticized *indigenismo*—was the
route to insure the emergence of a popular State that would guarantee at
the same time 'national unity'" (142). This homogenizing strategy was
a vehicle to take control of the nation. The *criollo* minority wanted to
take the power from the African Mexican or mestizo majority. By
implanting the illusion of a super or "cosmic race," which everyone
belonged to, the *criollos*, which already had the power of the Spanish
language at hand, would gain and monopolize power by promoting the
idea that everyone had a common past. Suddenly—as if by magic—
Cuauhtémoc and Moctezuma were made their "cultural" ancestors.

Monsiváis said that in the 40s Vasconcelos, worn out and petrified by
an ideological precipice, was supporting dictatorships such as Franco's
in Spain, and thereafter became a symbol for the extreme right. He also
points out that, therefore, the reconsideration of his works has been
made difficult (*Notas* 1428). Nevertheless, the following reading of *La
raza* reveals that Vasconcelos' views, at least since 1925, reflected the
same extreme right tendencies of two of the most influential Latin
American "homegrown racists" who adopted, with extreme ease,
European versions of racism, namely, Carlos Octavio Bunge and José
Ingenieros (Jackson, *The Black* 36).

Two points should be emphasized: Vasconcelos belonged to a string
of influential eugenicist thinkers of his time; and opposing thinkers,
such as José Joaquín Fernández de Lizardi (1776- 1827), among many
others, were accessible to Vasconcelos for his illumination. Therefore,
Vasconcelos' philosophy cannot be dismissed on the grounds of being
"a product of his time" since the lens for him to see beyond the colors
he chose, and induced a whole nation to choose, were at his disposal at
least since the publication of *El Periquillo Sarniento* (*The Mangy
Parrot*) (1816).

At first glance, *La raza* is a manifesto in defense of humanity, a
declaration based on the concept of universality full of love and
understanding for the oppressed. When viewed under Jackson's lens
on white aesthetics, it is apparent that Vasconcelos' understanding of
universality is intolerant of diversity.[25] He rejects the concept of a sum

of parts forming a whole. Instead, he sees a whole made-up by the disintegration, assimilation, eradication, or homogenization of the culturally diversity comprising Mexicaness[26] at the time he is formulating his doctrine.

Vasconcelos named his higher "race," "the cosmic race." According to him, this "cosmic being" would result from the natural and voluntary mixing of the best traits of all "races." Vasconcelos' "new race" would be superior to all known "races" (14-15). He claimed that love, specifically Christian love, was the foundation of his program (35). According to Santiago Castro Gómez: while "Idealizing *mestizaje*, Vasconcelos speaks of a 'cosmic race' that will unify the planet in a community ruled by voluntary union, harmony and beauty." Castro places him among late nineteenth and early twentieth century modernists, like Leopoldo Lugones and José Enrique Rodó, who exalted the aesthetic values of the "Latin culture," sharing this romantic eagerness for unity, happiness and redemption (141).

Vasconcelos utilized the first forty pages of *La raza* to spell out his doctrine of a superior being comprised of what he calls "the fifth race" or "the cosmic race." He began by explaining his theory of the evolution of the human species. He believed that "a race developed, and after progressing and decaying was substituted by another" (2). According to him, there had been four stages of human development: the "black" man in the beginning of the process; in the second stage a "red" man; in his third stage a "yellow" man; and in the fourth, or most advanced, stage the "white" man (1). This posture echoes the Frenchman, Joseph Arthur Gobineau's views (1855) on the hierarchy of "races:" white, yellow and black. According to Gobineau, only the "white or 'Aryan' race, [his supposed] creator of civilization, possessed the supreme human virtues of love of freedom and honor... His essay was used by the Nazis as proof of their racial supremacy" (Simon 1).

Vasconcelos divided white people into Saxons and Latinos, the former represented by English and Dutch, the latter by Spanish and Portuguese. He conceded that Saxons have the political and economical control of the Americas, and used part of *La raza*'s pages to issue a call for Latin Americans to transcend their political divisionism, of Saxon creation according to him, and to unite to confront the Saxons (4-8). Castro explains:

> In Vasconcelos we find also an identification of the "Latin spirit,"
> characteristic in Hispanic America, with the intuition of life, with feeling,
> with the irrational and beauty. [Vasconcelos] affirms that while the Saxon

civilization is founded on human dominance over the material world, in Latin America a race of synthesis is being formed that will seek the orientation of its conduct, not with pragmatic reason, but rather in feeling and love. Such a contrast between "Latin" and "Anglo-Saxon" symbolizes, at the bottom, the opposition between order (embodied in the idealism of the Hispanic-catholic culture) and "chaos" (embodied in the North American pragmatism and voluntarism), where order is understood as a synonym of harmony, and "chaos" as a synonym of "dissonance." In this manner a social imaginary is created where society and culture are governed by ideals of universality and consonance. (131)

Vasconcelos' pseudoscientific theory of "racial" evolution is a contradiction of contemporary scientific evidence. According to Luz María Martínez Montiel, the existence of humanity can be traced back two and a half million years:

The history of Africa in its beginning is the history of the appearance and evolution of man, the development of human groups, their dispersion and the formation of societies whose way of life, technical inventions, traditions and cultures have a significant place in universal history. Its importance is definitive among the rest of the nations and peoples of the world; notwithstanding, that history is little known. (*Negros* 25)

José Vasconcelos was unable to conceive that all human groups including those present in Mexico actually are, all and each one, the product of millions of years of evolution of the *Homo sapiens* species.

Vasconcelos proposed in *La raza* a type of *mestizaje* that was supposed to have allowed what he called "inferior races" to transcend their biological, social and spiritual condition. Pointing out similar characteristics of inherent superiority, Jackson denotes two patterns in Latin American ethnic relations. The first, a "pattern characterized largely by white racism, slavery and racial oppression..." found wherever there are or there have been black women and men. The second "is embodied in the concept of miscegenation or *mestizaje*, a process that, while loosely defined as ethnic and cultural fusion, is often understood to mean the physical, spiritual and cultural rape of black people" (*The Black* 1).

Moreover, in his study of African Mexico, Patrick Carroll states that:

given their slave condition, their ethnic group and color, the Spanish saw Africans and their descendants, whether enslaved or free, with their discernible physical characteristics, as inferior. Indians also found reasons

to limit their contact with black Americans, identifying them, just as
Spanish did, as foreigners based on race and ethnic group. (432)

Carroll explains that "the Catholic church supported secular authorities
in maintaining the system of *castas*..." and by studying marriage
records reports that in the sixteenth and seventeeth centuries he found
that white women, although still relatively few, " would hardly marry
outside of their racial group" (413), and that during the same periods
white men, "abided by the racist and ethnocentric social order" with
few of them marrying outside of their racial group" (415).

According to Vasconcelos, the "fifth universal race, fruit of the ones
before, and betterment of the past ones" (4) was supposed to trace its
origins in "the abundance of love that allowed the Spaniards to create a
new race with Indians and blacks" (14). While it is true that there was
a wide process of amalgamation of various human ethnicities in
Mexico, most of the mixing of whites with Amerindians or *castas* took
place outside of wedlock, for the marriage records and the physical
characteristics of the Mexican population are contradictory.

On the one hand, Spaniards would seldom marry outside of their
group and, when they did, it was with *criollos* or, as a last resort, with
"Euro-mestizos," or mestizos who appeared white. On the other hand,
according to Aguirre Beltrán, by 1570 the growing mestizo population
in New Spain reflects a greater amount of mixing activity outside of
matrimony between the Spanish, the Indian, and *castas* populations
(210). This indicates that mixing between whites and their supposed
inferiors took place more than what was officially accepted, and that
bastard[27] children or "*hijos de la chingada*" (sons of bitches) were
walking around everywhere as living proof of their fathers' actions. In
further support of this, Enrique Florescano has said:

> Even when the *castas* were numerically and socially important from the
> middle of the 16th century, they are almost not registered in that century or
> in the following. Since they were offspring of non-formalized sexual
> relations, they had a concealed or disguised social life. This group came
> to be the more discriminated by written and non-written laws, and the
> greatest social prejudices were concentrated against them. (211)

Was that the result of love? According to Martín Luis Guzmán, who
knew Vasconcelos personally, "this Spanish man that Vasconcelos
describes (and whom we can speak of with total frankness because we
are all a reference to him) is so non-existent and arbitrary that, page-by-

page, the history of Hispanicism denies it" (1402).

Vasconcelos' understanding of history and worldview did not end there. He also mentioned "Chinese who reproduce as mice" which, according to him, is "proof of lower zoological instincts;" he sympathized with and justified the rejection of this "race" by "the superior ones" (17). His charge against Asians continued when he described, "the Mongol with the mystery of his oblique eye, that sees all in accordance with a strange angle" (19). According to José Jorge Gómez Izquierdo, "xenophobia and racism acquired a presence in the ideology of the Revolution from its onset. This ideology helped to create the sense of national identity among Mexicans" (88).

Jackson draws attention to the fact that negative images of dark skinned people "reflecting nineteenth century mentality on race, surprisingly, have not been completely discarded in the twentieth century" (*The Black* 36). Furthermore, this ideology in post-revolutionary Mexico, beyond being embraced, was disseminated; it was used as a foundation in the making of "the modern social order" (Carroll 403). Jackson points out that the negative opinions "of New World intellectuals" are inherited from "the old prejudices of the colonial ruling classes" that had these intellectuals "convinced of the inferiority of the dark races" (*The Black* 36).

Vasconcelos portrayed blacks as "eager for sensual happiness, inebriated with dances and wild lust," while he presents whites as having a "clear mind... similar to their complexion and their fantasies" (19). The sensuality ascribed to blacks, the dance and lust, are examples of "preconceptions, misconceptions and stereotypes" that "while giving false if not one-sided images of the black, at the same time help indicate racist feelings toward black people among Latin-American authors." They are prejudices that, beyond damaging the black image, perpetuate the myths that "depict blacks as an inferior jungle beast, a provider of [entertainment]" (*The Black* 45, 46). Vasconcelos' literary representation of whites, blacks and others evokes the two separate worlds that developed in Mexico after the arrival of the Spanish. Ted Vincent's description of these worlds helps explain further how mentalities, such as Vasconcelos,' were formed:

> The Mexican elite had mansions, a university, monasteries, numerous cities to visit in, great governmental buildings to hang out in, and had the bishop's cloister for social teas and poetry readings. A tight and exclusive circle of wealthy whites and their lackeys hid in the mansions drinking Spanish wine, eating "white" bread, and practicing the 'Minuet.' Out in

the town square, the dark-hued people created Mexico, with tequila, tortillas and *La Bamba*. (5)

Bans were issued on musical expressions from the beginning to the end of the Colonial period because they "allegedly caused delinquent behavior and exhibited licentious African body movements" (Vincent 5). Arturo Melgoza says, "we know that blacks would gather in the central square of Mexico City to sing and dance...." He allows the reader to perceive the cultural value of the African manifestations of self-consciousness in Mexico (73), something that José Vasconcelos failed to understand.

Vasconcelos accepted what he called "the higher ideals of white men" (23) and envisioned that "perhaps among all characters of the fifth race white characters will dominate." He explained also "such a supremacy must be the fruit of free election" (23). His subscription to the bleaching out of dark people is evident when he said, "In the Iberoamerican world... we have very few blacks and the majority of them have been transformed already into mulatto populations" and that "the Indian is a good bridge for *mestizaje*" (25).

Vasconcelos' white aesthetics, found in the literature of other parts of the Americas, materialize when he asks, "why should it matter that all races mix if ugliness will find no cradle?" He predicted that in his utopian nation-state "the poverty, the defective education, the scarcity of beautiful types, the misery that turns people ugly," would all disappear (29). He explained that if up to his time there had been no great improvement of the species, it was due to the living conditions of "agglomeration and misery, where it has not been possible for the free instinct of beauty to work." He believed that "reproduction has been carried out like beasts without limit in quantity and without aspiration for improvement" and to satisfy the sexual appetite in any way possible while ignoring the spirit (30).

Vasconcelos thought very little of the mixing that had taken place for over four centuries in Mexico, as well as in other places, up to the post-Revolutionary era. This is apparent when he says, "we are not in a position to even imagine the modalities and the effects of a series of interbreeding truly inspired." He believed that "unions founded in the capacity and the beauty of the type, would have to produce a great number of individuals gifted with the dominant qualities." Vasconcelos saw them "electing immediately, not through reflection but by taste, the qualities that [he] wish[es] to predominate." He was certain that "the recessive offspring would not unite among themselves, but instead would search for quick improvement or would extinguish voluntarily all its desire to reproduce physically." He expounded, "from this, the black man, for example, could be redeemed; and little by little, by voluntary extinction the ugliest types [all non-'White' people] would give way to the more beautiful" (29-31).

In Vasconcelos' view:

> the inferior races, after becoming educated, would be less prolific, and the better specimens will ascend in a scale of ethnic improvement whose ultimate type is not precisely the white man but a new race that whites themselves would have to aspire to be in order to conquer the synthesis. (31)

In Vasconcelos' model "the Indian, by hybridizing with his related race, would jump the thousands of years that mediate between Atlantis [where they originate, according to his theory] and our epoch" (31). He believed that "in a few decades of eugenic aesthetics blacks could disappear along with those types marked by [his idea of] beauty as fundamentally recessive [and therefore] unworthy of reproduction" (30-31).

Vasconcelos' doctrine for *mestizaje*, as depicted above, was based on the extinction of what he saw as lower types of humans. However, he explained clearly that his theory differed from "brutal Darwinist selection" due to the fact that "interracial" mixing in his model would be a result of taste (31). In his doctrine, he found justification for his perspective because he was willing to mix with other "races," while the English would not dare because they "think blacks are a species closer to apes than to white man" (32). He taught, "every ascending culture needs to construct its own philosophy." He saw himself as the philosopher of Mexico and charged that "we have been educated under the humiliating influence of a philosophy developed by our enemies," and that because of it "we ourselves have come to believe in the inferiority of the mestizo, in the non redemption of the Indian, in the condemnation of blacks, in the irreparable decadence of Orientals" (33).

Vasconcelos proposed the need to "reconstruct our ideology and organize according to a new ethnic doctrine our continental life as a whole" (33). He underlined that "Christianity frees and engenders life because it contains a universal revelation in itself" and sees Jesus Christ as "the author of the greatest movement in history" (34). There are two points to be emphasized here. Vasconcelos, still a symbol of a secular revolution, promoted religion through education although it had been constitutionally banned in Mexico since 1857 after the Reform War. Also, the *Cristero* war (1924-1929) was brewing during the time of his conceptions in *La raza*, and his thinking could not be construed as helping the side he represented.[28] Vasconcelos saw "Christianity consummated not in the souls but in the roots of beings" (37).

Vasconcelos believed that all factors needed for his "fifth race" were present in the Iberian part of the continent alone, namely: spirit, "race," and land. He explained that there and then "the universal era of humanity could be started" because the "Nordic man, master of action," was present along with "the black man with a reserve of potentialities that come from the remote days of *Lemuria*"[29] (39) and "the Indian who saw Atlantis perish but who keeps a quiet mystery in his conscience" (39). Vasconcelos thought that all peoples and all abilities were there and that the one thing lacking was "the true love to organize and set on its way the law of history..." to create "the first universal culture, truly cosmic" (39).

Vasconcelos' views on *mestizaje* have started to be questioned recently as a result of the Civil Rights, Black is Beautiful, and Chicano Power movements in the United States, the Cuban Revolution and other no less important movements in favor of a black identity throughout the Americas and the world. This can be observed where Carroll mentions that there are two ways to understand how blacks were "almost forgotten" even when "their descendants supplied one of the greatest—if not the principal proportionally speaking— contributions to the *mestizaje*" (404). He analyzed African Mexicans in Veracruz and concluded, "An initial analysis of Afroveracruzanos suggests that their role, active or proactive, in the process of social interweaving between whites and Indians, eventually drove them to become almost racially and ethnically extinct." But Carroll points out:

> a more detailed analysis offers an alternative reading of history; the *Afroveracruzanos'* mediating vision helped in creating a social order of *castas*. This new social system did not predominate in central Veracruz or in the rest of the nation until the end of the XIX century, when the *castas* came close to the status of majority among the general population. The modifications/ mediations of the black Americans left a heritage in the region, which evolved before the persistent social and legal pressures from Spanish and Indians against them. (436-37)

Carroll also raises the question as to whether Veracruz' situation may be typical of the Mexican nation as a whole or just a sum of rare regional variants in the evolution of Mexico's *mestizaje*, and concludes that the case in Veracruz is typical of the role played by African Mexicans in the process of *mestizaje* in New Spain (429).

In terms of how the Africaness of the Mexican was finally erased officially from memory after the Revolution, Juan Carlos Ramérez Pimienta's comments, unknowingly, offer an interesting insight:

> [E]ducation is going to become one of the main factors for cohesion in post-revolutionary Mexico. In fact almost immediately at the end of the armed phase of the Revolution Alvaro Obregón appoints José Vasconcelos as the Minister of Education. He starts immediately an ambitious literacy campaign. The object—says Heuer—is to bring spiritually closer all groups in the country, that is to say, homogenize Mexicans by giving them a federalized education, in other words, the same history, with the same heroes, same past and the same country to sacrifice for. (217)

Vasconcelos' doctrine regarding a *mestizaje* creator of a cosmic man, in fact, masked Mexico's heterogeneity. This doctrine, while supposedly aimed at bringing everybody to an illusory mainstream, in truth was targeted at doing the opposite. His ideology was put into practice through an all-out government campaign to create one country through education, art, and mass media: "Vasconcelos was the first to capture and realize, while being minister [of education] the functional concept that modern aesthetics has found in the phenomenon of mural painting and on the diffusion of music for the humble Mexican masses" (Bar 76). This campaign blurred all Mexicans who were not white enough from the nation-state project[30] particularly the *mezclas*, *castas* or African Mexicans who nevertheless were the majority.

The mestizos who did not look white enough lacked representation in cinematography during the first half of the twentieth century. In this manner, they were made invisible and cast out of the ideal mestizo image through one of the most popular means of mass persuasion. Jackson cites Richard Pattee as pointing out that "[o]ne of the most interesting cases of the Negro in Latin America is the Negro that no longer exists" (*The Black* 3). Moreover, white looking mestizo actors like Pedro Armendáriz and Ignacio López Tarso acted the most famous parts of Mexican Amerindian images in cinema.

Ramérez asks: "is it possible to think that the PRI-government[31] did not design and implement a cultural policy to help it stay in power?"

He explains: "[w]e can think that this project is only a manifestation, the most important perhaps, the branch of a nationalistic unifying intention that as well covers literature and the plastic arts" (Ramérez 211).[32] At the end of his essay, Ramérez inquires whether Mexico's homogenizing policy worked, and responds: "Yes, to a certain point although it started falling apart during the sixties[33] and the student revolt." He also points out that the late Zapatista rebellion in Chiapas (1994-) is proof of "great sectors [of the population] that were never part of the national project" (221).

Dark African Mexicans, once out of sight, were soon forgotten.[34] And all of the blacks that appeared to be Euro-mestizos or Indo-mestizos quickly learned to deny their African heritage. María Teresa Sepúlveda's 1983 ethnohistorical work is an example of the far-reaching effects of Vasconcelos' policy of the 20s. She professes:

[t]he black, ripped naked from his region of origin, was unable to construct in New Spain the culture he belonged to; being a minority he was soon forced to mix biologically and culturally with the indigenous and mestizos adopting behavioral patterns from these groups. (101)

Sepúlveda acknowledges that in cases where blacks were really isolated they were able to keep some of their African cultural features, but she erases them physically from the population and finds that Mexico inherited from black Africa only some magical beliefs (101-03). She disseminates another two-pronged myth when she proposes that blacks were "imported," due to their physical strength, to do the work that "frail" Indians could not do. On one hand, it should be asked how the fierce warriors encountered by the Spaniards became "frail"? Was it not the inhuman treatment received and the imported diseases that nearly extinguished the Amerindian population? (Galeano 58-59; McCaa 11-14). On the other hand, as far as the black man's strength is concerned, Aguirre Beltrán explains:

When it was a matter of justifying blacks' enslavement and their introduction to American lands, it was said that a black man was worth four Indians, meaning that the work effort of a black man was equivalent to that of four Indians. Later on it was even said that a black man could resist rougher work than the white man. In this manner, the myth of the black man's physical superiority over the Indian and the white man was established as a means of subjecting the black man to the most barbarous exploitation. (180)

Aguirre Beltrén emphasizes as well that blacks were capable of doing more work, not due to their blackness, but because they had been hand-picked for the task: the majority of African men and women brought to the "New World" during the Transatlantic Slave Trade were on average between the ages of 18 and 22 "the majority being 18" (180). These men were in the prime of physical strength due to both age and to the fact that the trader would normally pick the biggest and strongest among all to receive a better price. Even so, there was a 15% death rate in the ocean crossing, and once at the work site, because of the inhuman treatment, they would last an average of "7 to 15 years" (Aguirre Beltrán 180- 182). Thus, Sepúlveda's teachings, under new light, can now be seen to be influenced by José Vasconcelos' racist ideology on *mestizaje*.

But what happened to the African Mexican after Vasconcelos' ideology became a "reality?" In 1946, Aguirre Beltrán declared that in Mexico, "especially after the Revolution there [was] no racist consciousness." He argued that in the Mexican census the data on "race" [was] not collected because "it is the law," and because "in a hybrid population such as ours this data would be illusory." He pointed out that even the word "race" had the tendency " to disappear from the official terminology" (178).

The key to understanding what happened to dark African Mexicans after the Revolution can be found in two of Aguirre Beltrán's words: "law" and "official." The existence of a law and an official doctrine that made all Mexicans "equal" served only to mask what Aguirre Beltrán identified elsewhere as the genuine "racist thinking of the conqueror" (172), a white racist thinking adopted and cultivated for hundreds of years among the Mexican population at large. Regarding this dominant ideology in Mexico, José Revueltas explains:

> The rareness, the strangeness of the dominant ideology, already institutionalized as a whole in the Constitution of 1857, of laws and of juridical policies of the State, rests particularly on the fact that the great indigenous masses are kept cut off from it, they don't belong to it, they are 'foreign' to that national consciousness, yet to become a total historical auto-consciousness. (149)

Now, it is true that in Mexico since 1821, "the distinctions by color of the dermis disappeared officially" (Ochoa 38). Also, it can be said that the majority of the population in Mexico are mestizos, but only in the sense of describing humans whose genetic make-up is black

African, Amerindian and Spanish, among others. It is also true that among the population today there is still a preference for the mestizos who are viewed socially as white. A good example of this can be found in popular sayings such as "*la mona aunque se vista de seda, mona se queda*," (an ape dressed in silk, still is an ape), or "*cafre*," "*grifo*," and "*coyote*," among other words, concepts or ideas that, although today have additional significations, they still possess powerful racial overtones.

Another example can be found in the Mexican immigration laws where the history of white racism is well documented. For instance, a certain Francisco Pimentel is recorded as saying in 1866 that Mexico needed foreign colonization to "augment and improve" the country's population (González Navarro v. I, 500). Also, in the same source, public opposition to black immigrants is documented in the newspaper, *El Monitor Republicano*, where blacks are characterized as "lazier, dissolute, and less intelligent than the Indian;" while white people are said to be "the most active, the most intelligent, in one word the most civilized" (González Navarro v. II, 185).

Between 1926 and 1931, the immigration to Mexico of non-white workers was restricted and "justified with openly racist arguments;" it was officially declared in 1928 that "it was mandatory to improve the race through *mestizaje* and this could not be achieved by yoking Mexicans with individuals from insignificant lineage." A great effort was taken to impede the entrance of blacks under the light of this opinion (González Navarro v. III, 34). Perhaps the most illustrative example can be found in the images of the "Mexican prototype" found in movies, television, newspapers and magazines.[35]

The consequences of the racist mentality and the white aesthetic reflected in *La raza* have yet to be fully studied because, as Bartolomé highlights:

> Even today, and in spite of the pluralist discourse and rhetoric, the concrete ideological and political practice reproduces the constituted historical block and points toward the homogenization of diversity assuming that differences are a motive for inequality. One of the dramatic concrete consequences of this political model has been the destruction of a great number of native societies: [...] the cultural suicide called ethnocide. (29)

An ethnic relations policy that ignores, dilutes and/or makes people disappear at will has to be questioned at its roots. It must be traced through history in all forms of expression and/or means of mass persuasion, including literature (canonic and popular) and cinematography. This is to take place with the new tools provided by multidisciplinary perspectives inclusive of the black experience and the vision of the vanquished. All facts, including what has been kept silent or conveniently forgotten, must be exposed for a fully informed debate based on all evidence, no matter how shocking or disturbing.

Under existing legal and academic views, it should be clear that "what was considered a civilizing act, based on a universalistic humanism, now is practically definable as a major offense: ethnocide" (Bartolomé 28). The homogenizing activities started by Vasconcelos in the 20s, carried on by many others in Mexico until today, need to be investigated further to understand their consequences, that is, the manner in which they have affected and are affecting humanity directly and or indirectly. The African heritage of the Mexican population and its ethnic legacy is negated outright in Mexico and little known throughout the world. The African contributions to Mexicaness and to humanity as a whole by extension are yet to be recognized.

The black phobia and white aesthetics found in part of Mexican literature and the arts embraced officially and even academically, are part of a pattern in the Americas wherever there have been or there are black men and black women. This is why what is discussed here may not appear new and may even seem to be a "worn out issue." In Mexico, progress in the area of ethnic relations will be difficult unless a closer look is taken at the ongoing debate on ethnic relations in other parts of the Americas such as Brazil, Cuba and the United States, and among other countries where African descent populations are developing a sense of ethnic identity and a feeling of self-worth.

Mexico, by denying its roots, will sadly continue to be a case of mistaken identity. On the issue of diversity in Mexico, Victor Zúñiga explains that following the Revolution of 1910-1920, new forms of rhetorical inclusion of "minorities" were designed in Mexico: "the existence of a Mexican mosaic" was admitted, "but this didn't change substantially the nineteenth-century project for social balancing supported until today by the myth of *mestizaje*" (246).

Mexico's project for entering modernity, as far as it relates to its social and ethnic diversity, was nearsighted. It was developed upon nineteenth century beliefs: "it did not take into consideration the presence of the 'others'... an enormous number of Mexicans that do not fit into the official definition of the nation" (Zúñiga 247). Moreover,

Zúñiga continues:

> one of the most surprising characteristics of the historical and political discourse about the nation in Mexico is its marked resistance to considering openly the question of cultural, linguistic and ethnic differences. Until a very few years ago we lacked all types of juridical or political discourse, no matter how weak, about the question of differences. (248-149)

Rowe and Schelling, in dealing with the problem of identity in Brazil, point out how Gilbert Freyre's transformation of the mestizo and characterization of Brazil as a " 'racial democracy,' reinforced the ideal of whitening because it led to the widespread notion that Brazil's racial problems were being solved through ethnic integration, whose goal remained white civilization." They also explain that it was Abdias do Nacimento, an African Brazilian playwright, who pointed out that "a crucial consequence of the persistence of this ideal... [was] the absence of a significant black consciousness movement" that prevented the achievement of "racial" identification and thus self-determination. Rowe and Schelling highlight as well that in do Nascimento's view "concepts such as miscegenation, acculturation and assimilation are in fact euphemisms for the sexual exploitation of [African Brazilian] women and the gradual annihilation of [African Brazilian] culture" (Rowe 42).

In Cuba, the debate on African Cuban expression, and curiously enough "the dialogue" with the United States on the subject, exists. Cuba, as in the case of the United States, has fostered the academic literary study of its Africaness, and although it may be argued that there is still much to accomplish, what cannot be denied is that the African Cuban presence and literary contributions to Cuba's, and by extension to Latin America's, identity is a fact today.[36] Cuba's achievements in ethnic relations, despite allegations that it is lagging behind, could throw some light on the problem of ethnic relations in Mexico.

Moreover, the one hundred million African blacks of the *Maafa* or black holocaust and their offspring of all color shades, in general, had very similar experiences in the European colonies on this continent.[37] In all instances, they were enslaved, relegated to forced labor, and in all colonial societies there is extensive documentation about their use and sexual abuse. The Africans taken to the United States were no exception. African Americans of the United States are African mestizos as well, in the sense of having Amerindian and European blood in them, just as African Mexicans do.

One may ask: how is it that African Americans of the United States have developed a sense of identity and self worth, even when "mestizo-scholars" argue that Anglo-Saxon racism is the worst type? This, while the presence of people of African descent in Mexico is still being denied or dismissed by the prejudicial, absurd, and simplistic argument that chants in Mexico "we all are Mexicans." Is there a "better" type of racism? What will it take to implement international charters, constitutional laws, decrees, declarations, policies on paper that have been officially condemning racism in theory for some time? When and how will it be learned that racism is an attitude generated by sheer ignorance and that the idea upon which this attitude is based is a fallacy, a socially defined illusion, a fruit of a poisonous tree that has caused, and continues to cause, an intolerable level of human suffering?

A full answer to these questions is beyond the parameters of this chapter. However, and for the expressed purpose here, it may suffice to say that while people who respond to that mentality in Latin America were and have been engaged in "confusionist" ideologies like Vasconcelos' negative *mestizaje*, trying to bleach out its black populations, their Northern counterparts had a clearly marked apartheid system, a system that even today collects census based on "race,"[38] where all African Americans and African American-mestizos of all shades of color are grouped together, paradoxically, making them a very visible "minority."

It was precisely this apartheid system that forced African Americans in the United States to look into themselves in search of identity, as there was no hope of entering the mainstream. Langston Hughes (1902-1967), explains that "In the case of the Negro [in USA] of course we have been free for one hundred years, but aren't integrated to democracy...[and he points out that] people who are apart from the mainstream of life develop... ways of their own" (Voices). These views, the African American experience in the United States, are clearly reflected in United States African American literature, music, dance, and cinematography, among other genres, with a voice universally known today. The presence of United States African Americans is irrefutably visible in the world nowadays.

And what is the connection of the above with the African Mexican situation? What if African Mexicans just want to see themselves as Mexicans, period? What if they are content with things as they are? It is the premise of this work that all humans as individuals are equal and have an equal right to self-determination. The arguments that "there are relatively few mestizos in Mexico with African characteristics left today" and that "they are on their way to extinction," or are "undergoing a process of integration," are not sufficiently valid in themselves to continue disenfranchising a single person in Mexico. It is anti-constitutional to do so and violates the United Nations Charter on Human Rights. Moreover, to allow materials like *La raza cósmica* to continue to circulate unchecked is inconsistent with the Modern Language Association's resolution of December 28, 1973, cited by Jackson, regarding "lingering racist ideas and materials" where the academic community is urged to "organize and support activities to... expose the anti-humanist and unscientific character of racist materials..." (*The Black* xiv).

The racist ideas spelled out in the prologue to Vasconcelos' *La raza* and contained in the rest of his memoirs fall clearly under the above-mentioned resolution. His white aesthetic and phobia of non-white people are worthy of study only as far as they open up a window to a world view that pervaded Mexico at the turn of the century and that still lingers today among many Mexicans who are yet to discover a truer picture of themselves. Given his influence, Vasconcelos must be studied in order to understand the process of disenfranchisement that so-called minorities, including African Mexicans, underwent as the homogenizing ideology behind *mestizaje* was put into practice and propagated through schools, art, and mass media channels of persuasion.

Notes

[1] In the *Pequeño Larousse* dictionary of the Spanish language, *mestizaje* is defined as the action and effects of adulterating or crossing races; it also defines a group of *mestizos* as those born to parents of different races. And "mestizo" is a synonym of bastard or hybrid. This is noted since from its inception the term is charged with negative connotations as do all terms that imply "impurity" of a sort or compare *Homo sapiens* to other animal species or plants. Mestizos are pure *Homo sapiens*. They certainly are not plants or any other type of animal species. Therefore, terms like "mulatto" or "hybrid" which have been used for naming the offspring of animals, or plants or other species would have also a derogatory effect.

Another point to be stressed is that in *Black Writers in Latin America,* Jackson cites two types of *mestizaje*: positive and negative, "the first means a blending of cultures in which there is equal respect for [all cultures]. The second means that a minority culture is absorbed as an inferior culture" (14). The negative type guides Vasconcelos' idea of *mestizaje.*

[2] As quoted by Richard L. Jackson (*The Black* 3).

[3] Patrick J. Carroll refers to him as "one of the earliest architects of the modern social order..." (403).

[4] For a full account on eugenics in Mexico and other Latin American countries see Nancy Leys Stephan's *The Hour of Eugenics: Race, Gender, and Nation in Latin America.* Ithaca: Cornell University Press, 1991.

[5] After a brilliant presentation of the political events that served to shape the modern nation, Knight concludes that Mexican intellectuals of the time were all practicing "reverse discrimination" whether by oppressing or by so-called defending the vanquished. What he fails to see is that, on one hand those in power to enact the racist project of nation, oppressors and self-appointed defenders, were generally the sons of Europeans born in America, the *criollos*; on the other hand what he sees as "reverse discrimination" is applied in a manner that could neutralize further debate regarding racism and therefore, racist practices and attitudes could not be debated leaving racism unchecked. It must be made clear that reverse discrimination would be possible presumably, if, and when, a group of the formerly called "inferior races" ascend to sovereign power and then justify the abuse to death of children, women and men, who share the same territory and time, on the basis of an idea of "otherness" such as that of "white supremacy."

[6] Carlos Monsiváis. "*Notas sobre la cultura mexicana en el siglo XX*." (1428). Full citation in bibliography.

[7] Echoing the words pronounced by Nelson Mandela, in 1962, during his trial in Pretoria, South Africa, it should be made clear that none of what is said here is based on personal considerations, but on important questions beyond the parameters of this work. It should also be mentioned that there will be references made to Eurocentric ideology and "white" people, and that terms such as "race," "black," "Amerindian," and "minorities," among other heavily charged social constructs, abstractions or "untruths," will be used. Despite the usage of these terms, from the outset it has to be reiterated that "I am not a racist and that I despise racism because I consider it a barbarous thing, whether it comes from a black man or a white man. However, the nature of this [work] forces the utilization of the terminology to be employed" (Mandela 19).

[8] Alan Knight, in "Racism, Revolution, and *Indigenismo*: Mexico 1910-1940," proposes that the commonly used category of "race" has been rightly questioned. However, he calls this category "a belief of great power"

deserving "analysis irrespective of [its] untruth" (75). This work subscribes to this premise.

[9] Populist movements were sweeping the continent. The states created during the colony were trying to become nations and the idea of "civilization," inherited from Europe, was equated with making all "minorities" into one homogeneous mass to the like of the leaders who either were *criollos* or people who believed as *criollos* did, that only white was beautiful.

[10] Patrick J. Carroll defines racism as: "a delineation and discrimination mainly based upon perceived physical characteristics, in particular the color of the skin...." (403). This definition is adopted in this study.

[11] African Mexican refers to persons of African descent, irrespective of their appearance, who constructed New World communities.

[12] Felipe Garrido coordinated the edition of two volumes under the title of *Lecciones de Historia de México*, (History Lessons of Mexico). They are particularly interesting because they are free texts from the ministry of education (SEP) utilized to teach incomplete information about African contributions to Mexicaness. And they are notable because they are utilized as a means to shape the imaginary of Mexican grammar school students today.

[13] In support of this, see the three following doctoral dissertations: Francis Daniel Althoff, Jr. "The Afro-Hispanic Speech of the Municipio of Cuajinicuilapa, Guerrero." U of Florida, 1998; Herman Lee Bennett. "Lovers, family and friends: The formation of Afro-Mexico, 1580-1810." Duke U, 1993; and Anita González-El Hilali. "Performing Mestizaje: Official Culture and Identity in Veracruz, Mexico." U of Wisconsin, 1997. Also see, "The Black Mexico Home Page" by Bobby Vaughn.

[14] Cecilia Rabell Romero defines *castas* as racial hybrids of black people of African descent (Carroll 431). This work adopts this definition.

[15] This is how the last name is spelled in the source.

[16] In a *post-scriptum* to a 1904 edition of *War and Peace*, Leo Tolstoy discusses how no individual alone makes the history of the life of nations (Tolstoy 429). This work subscribes to that view.

[17] According to Martín Luis Guzmán, Jorge Vera Estañol, Minister of Public Instruction in the later part of Díaz' dictatorship, wrote the "*Escuelas Rudimentarias*" 'rudimentary schools' project. Its purpose was: "to teach Castilian, the alphabet, and the fundamental rules of arithmetic to the *irredenta* indigenous class, particularly to those living away from civilized centers, in the mountains and in the country" (Guzmán 21). Vasconcelos receives recognition for his "ambitious campaign *Alfabeto, pan y jabón* [alphabet, bread and soap]" that basically is the twin of Vera Estañol's project (Garrido 2: 80). Agustín

Basave Benítez points out as well that Vasconcelos' ideology was influenced by his "good friend" Andrés Molina Enriquez, a *mestizófilo*: a scholar of Mexican *mestizaje* (Basave 72, 114).

[18] Garrido says that according to the population census of 1910, at the beginning of the Revolution there were more than fifteen million people and in 1921, following the Revolution the population was about fourteen million (2, 92).

[19] For a Eurocentric comprehensive account of the history of *mestizaje* in Mexico see Agustín Basave Benítez's *México Mestizo: Análisis del nacionalismo mexicano en torno a la mestizofilia de Andrés Molina Enriquez*. México, D.F.: Fondo, 1992.

[20] It is interesting to note that the former general, Porfirio Díaz, a Black Indian from Oaxaca who distinguished himself in the battle of Puebla against the French invasion during the Juárez government, despised his fellow Indians, called them "boys," became a positivist and a Francophile. Also, "Porfirian" prosperity did not reach the majority of the population. The millions of pesos [profit for concessions of natural resources made to England and France] were kept in the hands of an aristocracy (small in numbers and dressed in frock coats) and of a growing middle class (half a million members dressed with slacks and coats). Almost none of Mexico's wealth reached the masses who wore shirts and white indigenous *calzones"* (Garrido 2: 63).

[21] This colonial racial classification is explained in detail in Aguirre Beltrén's *La población*, 163-179.

[22] Ted Vincent notes that, "Mexico has a fourth race if one adds the descendants of the 100,000 Asian slaves brought to Mexico on the colonial Manila to Acapulco route. Since the law decreed that only Africans could be slaves, and the Spanish wanted more slaves, the Asians were declared Africans" (Vincent 2).

For a complementary study on racism and xenophobia against the Chinese part of the Asian population in Mexico see José Jorge Gómez Izquierdo's *El movimiento antichino en México (1871-1934)*. México, D.F.: INAH, 1991. It should be added that actually there were other racial and ethnic components.

[23] According to a recent unpublished commentary made by Richard L. Jackson "invisible" is a "key word all over Latin America" (November 1999).

[24] Reports on the number of visibly black Mexicans in the country as a whole vary from 200,000 to 600,000, and of course these numbers, arbitrary as they may be, do not include the millions of Mexican "blacks" who appear white, "Amerindian," or "mestizo" (Esteva-Fabregat 305). Even so, Colin A. Palmer expressed: "as their ancestors did, the few remaining persons who are visibly of

African descent continue to be productive members of society. But history has not been kind to the achievements of African peoples in Mexico. It is only within recent times that their lives have been studied and their contributions to Mexican society illuminated. Suffice it to say that contemporary black Mexicans can claim this proud legacy and draw strength from it..." (3).

[25] For a deeper insight beyond the issue here, see Martín Luis Guzmán's *Obras Completas* 1: 1399-1404,1443 where Miguel de Unamuno is quoted referring to Vasconcelos as a "confusionist."

[26] It may be interesting to point out that *Webster's New Collegiate Dictionary* and *Merriam-Webster* define "mestizo" in two totally different manners between the 1956 and 1995 editions. In 1956 mestizo is defined: "Esp. in Spanish America and the Philipines a person of mixed blood; esp., the offspring of a European and (East) Indian, Negro, or Malay; often, Phil. I., a person of Chinese and native blood." In 1995, citing 1582 as the year of the word's origin it defines: "a person of mixed blood; specif: a person of mixed European and American Indian ancestry."

[27] Basave Benítez points out that soon after the new "race" was being created "*mestizaje*" and "bastard" became synonyms (18).

[28] I thank my brother and colleague for reminding me that the *Universidad Nacional Autónoma de México, UNAM*, (The Mexican National Autonomous University) owes its logo—"*por mi raza hablará el espíritu*" (my spirit shall speak for my race)—to Vasconcelos.

[29] The Lemurs, mythological beings between Romans and Etruscans, were the ghosts of the dead. Interesting also is that lemurs are a subclass of primate mammals from Madagascar in Africa and from Malaysia. Ted Vincent relates that the black slaves from Asia came from Malaysia, New Guinea, and the southern Philippine Islands, including the island of *Negros* so named because the *Negritos* lived there (2).

[30] *Ethnologue Online* reports 295 languages in Mexico, one of which is Spanish (Grimes).

[31] PRI stands for *Partido Revolucionario Institucional* (Revolutionary Institutional Party). This party was in power continuously since the end of the armed phase of the Revolution of 1910-1920 until the year 2000 when Vicente Fox Quesada, from the rightist catholic *Partido de Acción Nacional* (National Action Party), won the elections.

[32] For a discussion on the "muralist art" as propaganda, see Melgoza's interview with Rufino Tamayo in *El crepúsculo de los últimos gigantes*. México, D.F.: SEP: Plaza y Valdés, 1989.

---

[33] Jackson has pointed out that during this period is "the advent of 'Black is Beautiful." It may be added as well that during those days some United States African American athletes during the 1968 Olympics in Mexico displayed "Black Power" by raising high their right hand fists covered with black gloves.

[34] For a greater insight in the workings of government propaganda see Chomsky's *Media Control: The Spectacular Achievements of Propaganda*. New York: Seven Stries, 1997 (1st ed, 1991).

[35] Alan Riding in *Distant Neighbors*, points out that: "half the models used on television are European or American [Caucasians], including many seductive blue-eyed blondes. In a country where less than 5 percent of the population is of pure Caucasian blood, the message is that things go better for white fair-haired 'foreigners'" (313). Also, on September 15, 1998, *Reforma*, a Mexican daily, published an add from "Herdez," a food Company, that says, "In September, live the happiness of tradition and paint your heart with our colors." The ad is a rectangle, the majority occupied by a tri-colored heart (green, white and red, the colors of the Mexican flag) with a photograph of a happy well-fed blond baby covering the center of the said heart (Viva). The relation nationality-blond is established thus.

[36] For one of the latest and most comprehensive studies on the subject see Edward J. Mullen's *Afro-Cuban Literature: Critical Junctures*. Westport: Greenwood Press, 1998.

[37] For a detailed account see Eduardo Galeano, *Las venas abiertas de América Latina*. México, D.F.: Siglo XXI, 1980 (53d ed.); Hugh Thomas, *Cuba or the Pursuit of Freedom*. New York: Da Capo, 1998 (1971 1st ed.); and Ronald Seagal, *The Black Diaspora*. New York: Farrar, Straus and Giroux, 1995.

[38] It should be mentioned that the classification of "Hispanic," that groups all people from south of the Río Bravo as a single "race" echoes the *criollo* deliberate indifference and insensibility to ethnic diversity. It is an imposition that denies the multiethnic make-up of the people arbitrarily grouped under said classification and it adds to the confusion.

Two

The Erased Africaness of Mexican Icons

> The mestizo dimension of our dance...
> originates from the encounter of the
> indigenous with the Spanish and the
> black.
> Gloria Contreras[1]
>
> *Jarocho*[2] dancing, particularly during
> the colonial period, was one of the
> expressive forums for the articulation
> of African cultural consciousness.
> Anita González El-Hilali

Mexicans speak various languages[3] and have a host of appearances as the result of hundreds of years of willing and forced amalgamation among people from Africa, America, Asia, and Europe. Mexicaness (*mestizaje*, "hybridization,"[4] or *mulataje*) is a merge of people and worldviews of all ages and places. Its known African, Amerindian, Asian, and European ethnicities are in themselves the result of previous ethnic blending. As with all known ethnicities, Mexicaness, a culture of cultures, has its own complex set of self-expressions that reinforce national identity.

The preceding chapter presented how African Mexicans were

psychologically "bleached out" or erased from national memory by an all-out government campaign of mass persuasion through public education and the arts, among other more traditional mass persuasion channels. It was exhibited that this strategy produced a narrative on nation exclusive of Mexican Africaness. It analyzed the *criollo* or white racism found in *La raza cósmica* and dealt with the "prejudice of not having prejudices,"[5] underlying *mestizaje*'s ideology and its dire consequences that reverberate throughout Mexico to this day and still "imprint a colonial hue on interethnic relations" (Bartolomé 300).

The present chapter explores the plagiarizing of African contributions to Mexicaness and their official propagation, worldwide as sacred emblems of Mexicaness, after their Africaness was narrated to disappearance. It discloses that various Mexican or mestizo popular cultural forms found in dance, song, food, and speech systematically omit, or no longer recognize their Africaness, rather claim to be expressions of Spanish and Amerindian origins (in that order). The *criollo* founders of the modern nation utilized the means at their disposal to erase: the fact that the Africans taken to Mexico (and other parts of the world) were transporters of ethnicities that had been developing at least two and a half million years; and that, albeit their hell or due to it, they modified their adopted environments with the power of ancestral voices that continue to speak their wisdom through what is being called popular cultural expressions.[6]

The study of the symbols of Mexican national identity is fundamental to lay the critical foundation to discern the Africaness of *mestizaje* in this chapter, as well as in ensuing chapters, and future works (including how visibly black Mexicans are caricatured in comics).[7] This will help to exhibit how the "cleansing" of Africaness occurred and the detrimental effects it has on a national identity that while promoting itself as "family oriented" forces Mexicans to negate their own African genes.

To this end, immediately after introducing the perspective on popular cultures to be adopted, a brief look will be given to three of the ethnic components involved in the configuration of Mexicaness: the African, the American, and the European civilizations. It will be shown how the pertinent cultures from the civilizations involved in Mexican *mestizaje* were mestizo cultures themselves prior to coming together in "New Spain."

Subsequently, the development of the originally African Mexican *jarocho* dancing and singing from Veracruz will be analyzed, as well as its influence on: (1) the *sones*[8] of Costa Chica, a southern Pacific coastal zone, located in the states of Guerrero and Oaxaca; and (2) the *mariachi* song and dance from "a region in western Mexico that includes the states of Jalisco, Nayarit, Zacatecas, Aguascalientes, Guanajuato, Michoacan, and Colima; a region extending as far north as Sinaloa and Durango and as far south as Guerrero" (Clark 1). The *jarocho* and the *mariachi* personification are two of the national icons of Mexicaness in and outside of the country. These characters and their supposed behavior appear in literary works such as Manuel Payno's *Los bandidos de Río Frío*, *El Zarco* by Ignacio Manuel Altamirano, *Astucia: el jefe de los hermanos de la hoja o los charros contrabandistas de la rama*, by Luis Gonzaga Inclán, and *Calvario y Tabor* by Vicente Riva Palacio, that are yet to be read under Jackson's lens.

Next, the origins of *menudo* or " tripe stew" (at times made with chitlins and other entrails) which appears in *La vida inútil de Pito Pérez* (Romero 13) will be traced to expose partial translations that further detach this popular cultural expression from its Africaness such as Cord's translation of *menudo* simply as "stew" (4) or as "meal" (87). *Menudo* stew is an offspring of Congo's *mondongo*, and in its "mestizo" form is a typical dish found wherever there are *mariachis, jarochos* or *fandangos*.

Finally, the originally Bantu verb *chingar* will be analyzed as a word that makes Mexican Spanish, and many of its popular forms, unique.[9] *Chingar*, as is common knowledge, is one of the most representative popular forms of speech. Understanding the African genesis of this piece of "poetry," as Octavio Paz calls it, together with other pieces of the puzzle mentioned above, allows the decoding of the white aesthetics of literary works, such as: *El perfil del hombre y la cultura en México*, *El laberinto de la soledad*, and *La muerte de Artemio Cruz*, among other pillars of the modern nation, from a perspective inclusive of the black experience. This reattaches, across the continent and beyond Eurocentrically devised barriers, the Africaness of Mexicaness; and reinserts Mexico within the Caribbean experience and consequently the *Maafa*.

According to Rowe and Schelling, mass culture ["cinema, radio, comics, *fotonovelas*[10] and, above all, television" (7)] and popular culture are not the same. However, they recognize their interrelation and explain: "[w]hen the popular is defined not as an object, a meaning or a social group, but as a site —or, more accurately, a series of dispersed sites— then it generates a principle of opposition to the idea, imposed by authoritarian liberalism or by populism, of the nation as a single body." They also emphasize, "The notion of dispersed sites is not the same as pluralism." In pluralism the state is given a "neutral" place and this cannot be said about societies (as in the case of Mexico) where the state "homogenize[d] culture in order to consolidate the power of the ruling classes." Rowe and Schelling point out that "culture is inseparable from relationships of power" (10).[11]

Luz María Martínez Montiel, in *Negros en América*, states that the Iron Age preceded the Bronze Age in Africa. Africa is scientifically understood as the cradle of humanity and civilization. Regarding communication, she explains:

> During thousands of millennia Africa did not have writing. The means of narrative and ideological expression were unknown; yet the constant process of emotional thinking is recorded. This is the reason why the African, from pre-historical times, produces engravings, paintings, music and dance that are akin to visual or auditory dynamics that manifest, beyond an idea, human emotions. (38)

She also explains that aside from the Egyptian, all other African systems of communication, at the time the Transatlantic Slave Trade took place, were based on corporal and emotional expressions or non-verbal communication (39). It is paramount to keep this in mind to recognize that enslaved Africans, as all humans, were cultural entities and that as such, they defended their identities. Furthermore, the cultural texts or oraliture contained in African dances and songs, and in the dances and songs that developed from their exchanges with other ethnic groups, hold a non-verbal maroon Carnival voice that, in the case of Mexico, has yet to be heard.

The African people brought to New Spain starting in the middle of the sixteenth century, according to Aguirre Beltrán, included "white slaves," "slaves from the Levant" and "black slaves" principally from a three to four hundred kilometer strip located in the coastal region of West Africa between the Senegal and Coanza rivers (102-104). The "white slaves" were the people taken in the war against Islam. The greater part (of these people) was from Morocco: "Moors, Berbers, Jewish and *Loros* that came to the Western Indies accompanying their masters...." (104). The Catholic Church forbade the entrance of these "infidels" to the Spanish colony in America in the sixteenth century (although this interdiction was not always respected).

The Berbers are known to be one of the earliest settlers of North Africa in "Tripoli, Tunisia, and Algeria and are said to be descendants of the ancient Libyans" (Aguirre Beltrán 104). The Libyans throughout the centuries received "biological and cultural contributions from the Phoenicians first, then from the Arabs, and later from the blacks in different proportions." The Moors are also the result of the mixing of various groups of people who "entered in contact with blacks [and] absorbed a considerable quantity of color" (Aguirre Beltrán 104-05). The "true black" people (the majority of slaves brought to New Spain) were themselves mestizos of mestizos, a result of the amalgamation of diverse black African peoples and cultures, or of black African and Arab, or of European and African peoples and cultures. For instance, Aguirre Beltrán mentions the Fula, a people originally Caucasoid who, after mixing, had become predominantly black and who were mistaken for Mandingos when brought to the colony (110). The number of ethnic groups these people came from is too large to mention here, but suffice it to say, most Africans came from Guinea, Sierra Leone, and São Jorge da Mina, São Thome, and Manicongo.[12]

The "European" colonial component of Mexican *mestizaje* comes predominantly from Northern Africa, the Iberian Peninsula, and has an Asian heritage as well. To dispel the confusion, a brief discussion of the history of the various peoples and cultures that populated the Iberian region from its origins until the invasion of America will follow. John A. Crow states that the Iberians, "a small, wiry, dark-complexioned race... probably began to arrive in Spain from northern Africa around 3000 B.C." (24). About the twelfth century B.C.E., the "Phoenicians, a Semitic race of the Canaanite branch" began doing business in the area. They are said to have founded the port cities of Cadiz and Malaga (25).

Approximately 900 B.C.E., the Celts, a Nordic people, began to arrive and settle in the north of the Iberian Peninsula. The Greeks came to Spain at about 600 B.C.E., "they came first as traders but later established several trading posts mainly along the Mediterranean coast... and also possibly along the northern Cantabrian shores" (Crow 26). In the third century B.C.E., the powerful Phoenicians from Carthage, in North Africa, invaded Spain under the leadership of Hamilcar Barca. Barcelona derives its name from him, and Cartagena is a legacy of this period. By 205 B.C.E., the last Carthaginians were forced out by the Romans and returned to Africa.

The Romans dominated and colonized Spain and by 19 B.C.E. "Hispania...became the granary of Rome and the wealthiest province of the empire" (Crow 29). The Roman Empire itself was a mosaic of people and cultures extending from parts of today's England to northern Africa and parts of Asia. In the fifth century, the Germanic warlike Visigoths conquered Hispania, a place peopled by Vandals, Suevi, and Alani who had invaded the peninsula in 409 A.C.E. The Visigoths, a semi-civilized people, forced the Vandals out of southern Spain and into North Africa, and dominated Spain until 711, when the Moors arrived from North Africa. The Moors stayed for the next eight hundred years. They brought no women along but took local women as spouses. Spain was born from the mixing of many peoples and many cultures. The Spanish mestizos that came to America were ethnically as African as they were European or Asian, and unless it is shown otherwise, history supports this perspective.

The Amerindian people of the land that became Mexico were as heterogeneous as the invaders and their slaves. And, although the differences among Amerindians are yet to be fully understood, the fact remains that in Mexico, there were many different thriving nations with long histories and large urban concentrations. There were people, such as the Aztecs, who had conquered and subjugated others, and whose empires covered vast areas by the time the European invaders and enslaved Africans and Asians arrived.

The history of the people of the area before their documented encounter with Europe, Africa and Asia is classified in three periods: The Formative, from approximately 2000 B.C.E. until 100 A.C.E.; The Classic, from about 100 A.C.E. until 900 A.C.E.; and The Post-Classic, from about 900 A.C.E. until the arrival of the new people. The Olmecs occupied the tropical lands of Veracruz from 1500 B.C.E. until 100 A.C.E. Their influence extended well into Central America and they left a vast cultural legacy. Their best-known pieces of artwork are "the eleven clossal Negroid heads in the Olmec heartland" (Van Sertima 31).[13]

The next period is marked by the culture that flourished in Teotihuacan with the descendants of the Olmecs between 300 and 600 A.C.E. and the Zapotecs, from about 500 A.C.E. until the arrival of the Spanish, Africans and Asians. The Zapotecs lived in Oaxaca. Between 800 A.C.E. and 1100 A.C.E., after the Teotihuacans' disappearance, the Nahuatl speaking Toltecs emerged. Tula, in today's Hidalgo, was their cultural center. Toltec architectural influence extended into southern

Mexico. Circa 900 A.C.E., six other groups of Nahuatlacans arrived in Central Mexico and, while they were settling their political boundaries, a seventh group left Aztlan. This group was "constituted in seven *calpullis* [clans]: the Yopicans, the Tlalcochalcans, the Huitznahuacans, the Chihuatecpanecans, the Tlacatecpanecans, the Izquitecans and the Aztecs. According to the Mexicayotl Chronicle, the god Huitzilopochtli gathered these seven clans and, before they left from their unknown place of origin to central Mexico, told them they were now Mexicans (Basañez 62).

After many wars and alliances with the people that had arrived before them, these Mexicans ended as prisoners of war and gained their freedom only after defeating the Xochimilcans and taking eight thousand ears from their prisoners to the Culhuacans in 1323. The Mexicans or Aztecs arrived in 1325 at the island in Lake Texcoco that became the center of their empire. Until just before the arrival of Hernán Cortés in 1519, the Aztec empire extended throughout all of central Mexico and as far south as northern Central America. "Only the domains of Michoacan, Tlaxcala, Metztitlan, Yopitzinco and Totepec remained independent from Mexico-Tenochtitlan" (Basañez 74).

The Mayans, the other advanced civilization of Mesoamerica, inhabited the southern region of Mexico and had a long history as well, but by the fifteenth century "the wars among Mayans and other groups led to their destruction and to the final decadence of their civilization" (Kattan-Ibarra 27). There were many other important nations in Mexico as well. Today, 56 groups of the descendants of the original Amerindians, comprising about 12 million people, have been identified (Zúñiga 247). They speak some 289 living languages (Grimes 1).

It must be emphasized that the "blood" of the pre-Colombian people referred to above runs in the veins of most of today's more than 100 million Mexicans (in Mexico and abroad) along with Spanish blood and African blood in various percentages.[14] According to Patrick Carroll, there are two ways of looking at this mix: there is the notion that the African element disappeared through *mestizaje* from the population at large, as José Vasconcelos and the people he represented professed. This notion is an example of *negative mestizaje*. On the other hand, "a more detailed analysis offers an alternative reading of history" which states "a long time after the end of the nineteenth century ... the *castas* were close to the status of majority among the general population." From this *positive mestizaje* perspective, Mexican mestizos—the overwhelming majority of Mexicans—are as African as they are anything else (436-37).

Ricardo Pérez Monfort refers to various local and foreign nineteenth century chroniclers describing the picture of a "*chinaco*" and a "*china*"[15] dancing the *jarabe* [16] as the image of a "typical Mexican fiesta" (23). Arturo Melgoza Paralizábal, in *El maravilloso monstruo alado* (*The Marvelous Winged Monster*), a book-length essay-interview with Gloria Contreras, states that the mestizo dimension of the popular dances that "people dance all over Mexico," originated at the meeting point of the Amerindian pre-Hispanic cultures, the Spanish cultures and the black African cultures (15, 17). Mexico is no exception in the Americas. The undeniable black African musical development inherent to nationalities all over the continent in every adopted language —*bomba, contradanza, cumbia, cumaná, charanga, guarachá*, jazz, *mambo, merengue, plena*, rhythm & blues (or as, it became known in its bleached out name, rock 'n' roll),[17] rumba, salsa, samba, *sandunga, socabón, son*, tango,[18] to mention a few— is also intrinsic to Mexicaness.

Many of the colonial dances cited by Melgoza had been mentioned in Pablo González Casanova's *Literatura perseguida en la crisis de la Colonia* (*Persecuted Literature During the Colony's Crisis*) as early as 1958. However, González Casanova's historical essay falls short of recognizing the Africaness of the music and songs mentioned. Nevertheless, the essay "Afrocuban: Music to Salsa" by Olavo Alén Rodriguez, and the collection of essays *Afrodescendientes: Sobre piel canela* (*Afro-descendants: About Cinnamon Color Skin*) by Álvaro Ochoa Serrano shed light on the Africaness of Mexican popular music forms.

Juan Rejano, after describing his short visit in the seventies to Yanga[19] and San Juan de la Punta (two Mexican towns in the Gulf of Mexico state of Veracruz where there are a large number of visibly black mestizos) points out that Mexicans have rhythm and know how to sing[20] (62-64). Rejano refers to various popular Mexican dances and songs and notes their "spice" and "flavor" but fails to recognize that the rhythm of the people and the songs and dances he is writing about derive from the Africaness of *mestizaje*.

This is not surprising if one considers that there have been few references to the topic and Mexicans have systematically avoided acknowledging their Africaness since the white aesthetic controls their social and psychic paradigms. The methodical practice of omitting the

Africaness of Mexicaness in modern times has yielded an insufficient identity narration,[21] the forging of a whitened image of the nation remote from its ethnic make-up, and a severe psychological dislocation among large sectors of the population who are unable to perceive the social precipice that separates them from the sought whiteness. It has prevented Mexicans from acquiring the sense of worth that other people of African heritage have conquered elsewhere in the Americas.

The national songs and dances studied here are performed cultural narratives or "ethnic texts." In referring to the intracultural means of expression and of communication of the subjugated, Hugo Niño points out the existence of a dynamic means for the sharing of culture whose:

> aesthetic is not exclusively verbal but total... It has a stylistics that passes through the verbal phase, but it really forms in its performance and in its capacity to process concepts. There is not only a style in the text: the final stylistic result of each one of the texts depends on the acting of the narrator, guided by the reception of the audience. In that moment the style of the text narrated is constituted and its efficacy and the authority of the narrator are recognized, not that of the text, since this depends on the community itself. (113-14)

Niño's approach to the ethnic text clarifies this African centered reading of Mexican songs and dances "with their connotation of ample popular participation" (Pérez Monfort 16). It allows postulating that the audiences had to be in tune, body and soul, with what was presented in order to participate to the extent they did; and to propose that if the ethnic texts were African in part, the people had to be as well in order for the style, authority and efficacy of the narrator, audience and text to be constituted, and reach the level of a political discourse that led the African Mexican nation to its emancipation and independence.

José Vasconcelos, known as "The Educator of Mexico" and "The Teacher of Latin American Youth," believed and professed that the *Gato* and *Bomba*, "famous pseudo-native dances" that he had heard in Yucatan, were "truly Spanish" (185). These dances are African Caribbean in origin. But paradoxically, his description is helpful to the task at hand:

> [they] are collective dances where the dance is suddenly interrupted by the *Bomba*. While others laugh in wonderment, a dance couple tells one another amorous complements in jest and in verse, before continuing to dance. The enchantment of the dancers' motion and the voluptuous joy of the melodies, combine to create a strong feeling of triumphant beauty.

> Someday this sensual, but vigorous and pure art form will go back from
> the rural areas to the cities to correct the sterile artifice, the degraded and
> poor lasciviousness of urban customs. (185)

González Casanova dedicates a full chapter to the "forbidden songs
and dances" that he identifies as the foundations of the Mexican
popular satire (82). He takes the reader back to the end of the
eighteenth century, and through an extensive analysis of documents
from the Spanish Inquisition, he reports on the persecution of the songs
and dances with which "blacks and mulattos, soldiers, sailors and the
broza [lowest classes] relax" (65). He mentions the *Chuchumbé*, and
other *sones* such as: *La maturranga; Pan de manteca; Toro Nuevo,
Toro viejo; El jarabe Gatuno; El Saranguandingo; Pan de jarabe; La
cosecha;* and *Mambrú.* He interprets them as expressions that mock
religion and death (65).

These expressions were labeled "infernal" by the Inquisition,
society's censor then, and were also recognized as a type of song and
dance that "plagued" New Spain's central nervous system reaching the
high and the lowlands outside of Veracruz: Puebla, Celaya, Querétaro,
Pachuca, Pénjamo, Valladolid, and Salamanca.   Though short of
acknowledging the Africaness of the movement he studies, González
Casanova reports that the *Sacamandú* was brought to Veracruz by a
black man from Havana (69) and that these creations:

> of the happy unconscious, of the natural mayhem, of the naive provocation
> with which the authors of the first profane songs and dances worked,
> developed a challenging consciousness, a sought mayhem, a malicious
> provocation, hidden behind the anonymous roles and turned into a true
> satire. (82)

Ricardo Pérez Monfort adds a dimension to González Casanova's
perspective thirty-six years later.   After discussing the Mandingo
origins of the word *fandango* (the Mexican fiesta where the songs and
dances referred to are acted out or performed), Pérez Monfort explains
how "the *fandangos*, and in particular the dance of the *jarabe*, acquired
a connotation of protest, but also of identification" of having become
Mexican (22).

During the Mexican Independence movement, the insurgents would
insist on the performance of *casta* protest songs and dances in their
fiestas: if they were popular already "it was in independent Mexico that
they acquired an irrefutable card of nationality" (Pérez Monfort 22).[22]

Melgoza mentions that General Vicente Guerrero, one of the last leaders of the war of Independence and the president of Mexico from 1829 to 1830, "would be exposed publicly as a gambler and a ladies man and for going with enthusiastic regularity" to *fandangos* (24). Guerrero's social behavior can be understood if Mexican official history had not been deliberately forgetful of his African Mexican origins (Vincent 7).

According to Pérez Monfort, "From the Gulf Coast to the hot lands of the west, in the *Bajío* and in various states of the [Mexican] south, the *fandangos* gave free rein to popular creativity," they became the characteristic Mexican festive manifestations (23). Pérez Monfort also explains that in independent Mexico, these lyrics, dances and *sones* were "executed freely" and thus they became characteristic of the popular national identity and in time they generated the icon that determined a classic image of the Mexican nationality "the *chinaco* [today's *charro*] and the china dancing the *jarabe*" (23).

Ochoa describes the *fandango* and its origins and development in light of the Africanizing of Mexico (129-41). He clarifies that the *fandango* is a black *bailongo* (a gathering to eat, drink, and dance) adopted by whites and *descoloridos* (bleached out or mixed people). Ochoa informs that Rolando A. Pérez Fernández established the "Bantu, African linguistic and cultural origins of the *fandango* and its association with chaos"[23] (129). Ochoa recounts how the *fandango*, following its expropriation by the high spheres of the Spanish urban population, came and went between Africa, America and Europe during the colonial epoch or the "trafficking and transit" period, as he refers to it. Ochoa explains:

[the *fandango*] acquired a very particular twist in the Iberian Peninsula in plays and music—ballet-pantomime, comedy, spinets, sonatas—and became recognized as typically Iberian, and with this [false] copyright traveled parts of Europe and North America. (130)

The *fandango* in Mexico was a celebration, "an experience, and a variety show" that happened in open or closed areas in gathering places: "inns, eateries, patios and arcades." The *fandango* propagated in rural and urban areas alike. It created a stage "to solve differences, to manifest anger, to compete, to replenish [body and soul] and to enjoy [a moment of freedom];" it occurred "any day of the week, preferably Saturday, Sunday and holidays" from the seventeenth century on (Ochoa 134).

Ochoa also takes the reader to Veracruz—the port of entry for most of the people and cultures that came to Mexico during the colonial period—and relates a complaint made to the Inquisition: "in the narrow street called *La Campana*" two couples, men and women went out to perform the *Pan de manteca* dance. He cites another complaint from someone offended because in The *Plazuela* of *Santo Domingo* there was a *fandango* where "a contredanse was performed, women and men embracing and making lascivious movements." In the same part, Ochoa refers to a legal process against the mulatto, "Pablo José Loza, an artisan, for having sung and uttered stanzas and heretical sayings in a *fandango*, in the middle of the plaza, in the arcade of Villa de León" (134).

In *fandangos*, people sang and danced to "a musical tradition" called *son* (González-El 182). This musical tradition, according to Olavo Alén Rodríguez, "is, in fact, one of the musical styles or genres that may be considered genuinely Cuban from very early times, but never before the second half of the eighteenth century" (61). He states:

> The *son* lyrics became a mixture of the African way of expressing concepts—very complex images expressed in few words—and the meticulous descriptive style that the Spanish cultural heritage contributed to the popular speech of the Cuban population. (69)[24]

This African Cuban tradition constitutes the foundations of *jarocho* and *mariachi* song and dance. To trace its arrival in Mexico, Alén cites Argeliers León:

> The expansion of the *son* complex beyond its area of origin was helped along by the intense coastal trade that existed between Cartagena and Yucatán, and between the ports of southern Cuba—including the Isle of Pines—and Puerto Rico and the Dominican Republic. (63)

In addition, from the onset of the seventeenth century, Mexico engaged in trade with "Peru, Guatemala, Puerto Rico and Havana" (Reynoso 29). The *son* is an African Cuban tradition that spread throughout the Spanish colonies in America and went to Spain and its territories elsewhere. The *son* may have entered Mexico through Yucatán and Veracruz just as the aforementioned "*Sacamandú* [that] was brought to Veracruz by a black man from Havana..." (González Casanova 69). The *son* in Mexico was "first officially mentioned in 1766 'when inquisition authorities condemned a *son* called the

Chuchumbé on immoral and anticlerical grounds'" (González-El 182; and González Casanova 65).

The *son jarocho* is widely acknowledged as a folkloric musical genre representative of Veracruz and of Mexico:

> [It] developed from unique syncretistic performance styles common to field workers of [Amer]indian and African ancestry. Its acceptance by national cultural institutions as a mestizo art form is a post-Revolutionary phenomenon. During the colonial period *jarocho* dancing was associated with largely autonomous populations that lived in the coastal region of [Veracruz] and specifically with African and Native American slaves.... jarocho dancing, particularly during the colonial period was one of the expressive forums for the articulation of African cultural consciousness. (González-El Hilali 180)

González Casanova, referring to the above mentioned *Chuchumbé son* of 1766, says that the music of this dance, whose melodies and rhythms "indubitably belong to the Caribbean family,"[25] has not been preserved and that "only the stanzas, sung by the spectators while the others danced, are left" (65). These dances in their new environment absorbed other elements giving birth to the *son jarocho* sung by *jarocho* musicians and the *son ranchero* sung by *mariachi* bands, in other words, Mexican mestizo music. González Casanova further explains the *Chuchumbé son*:

> These stanzas could be one of many isolated manifestations of religious profanity, if from their birth there had not been other similar tendencies and if the edict with which they were prohibited had not been applied to the persecution of the multiple profane dances and songs that emerged at that time. (65)

González Casanova points out that they are unique "because they represent some of the most daring contempt of religion and death, and because they never abandon the delight of making sexual passes (with few exceptions) toward sacred things." He emphasizes that the stanzas: "Integrated into the brutality of the movements, the irreverent fantasy of the costumes, to the devilish climate created by the music and screams, formed a whole destined to break the harmony of sacred music, or of pious dances and songs" (65).

In mid nineteenth century, Manuel Payno describes from a *criollo* perspective what he calls a "colloquy" in a *palenque*[26] in Puebla. "A representation of the life of the Virgin, from the time she marries Saint

Joseph until the birth of Christ in Bethlehem." He was informed of this activity by "a great poster depicting devils throwing flames and other analogous figures" posted at the entrance to the arcade in the central plaza. Payno describes the audience as "a bronzed group of severe and very rare physiognomies [of whom the majority are] two social oddities... the *lépero* and the china."

Payno says that instead of watching the play, he is having a better time watching a group of people "eating raw eggs with salt and drinking huge swigs of *aguardiente* spirits while making comments on the representation and saying some crude adages." These skits, for Payno, are a ridiculous parody of the sacred story. According to him, there is violence acted, and the public roars with laughter at the insults, obscenity and foolish remarks about the "most poetic and tender part of the Catholic religion." He recalls nostalgically Calderón's *Autos sacramentales* and a different reception to the theme. Payno sees the play before him as highly immoral because "their only contribution is to ridicule the religious beliefs and to awaken singular doubts about the truths of dogma." The performance ends with "*jarabe* and *palomo* dances" (73-77).

Jarocho sones, as well as *mariachi sones*, are performed in *fandangos*. They are both based on a *zapateado* or *zapateo* (rhythmic footwork)[27] performed on a *tarima* (a wooden stage) in open or closed areas as in the case of the *mariachi*. "By definition, a *son* must be of 4/6 time, have an unlimited number of verses (each one of which is a complete thought unto itself), and be played for dancing." The *jarocho son*, however, has 4/6 and 4/4 time (Carraher 1). Hugh Thomas, reporting on the *bailes de tambor* (drum dances) in Cuba's sugar and coffee plantations of the mid nineteenth century, states, "in the country, the most customary dance was the *zapateo*, danced to the harp or guitar, but sung by all present too" (147). Moreover, according to Thomas, Fernando Ortiz points out:

> [...] the importance in Cuba too of Negro literary tournaments, entertainments rather than admittedly religious, long collective literary improvisations on specific themes, directed perhaps against some institution or person who had committed an offence against the Negro way of life. From these entertainments developed some of the specifically entertaining, that is, non-religious dances, such as the *rumba*....(521)

Other African Hispanic American forms of the *son* such as the Peruvian *zapateo* (*Perú: Música Negra*) show similarities that indicate related origins, but one important characteristic of the Mexican version of the *son* (with its regional varieties) is the routine use of the *tarima*:

> Though most people don't realize it, the *tarima* is another essential instrument. A *tarima* is a platform about a foot high, approximately the size of a piece of plywood and usually made of cedar planks. This is where the dancers pound out the rhythms, interacting with the musicians, sometimes following and sometimes dictating the direction of the music (...) the belief is that for the slaves, who were deprived of their drums, the *tarima* was the replacement. (Carraher 2)

In support of this, Ochoa, referring to the *fandango*, or *mariachi* in Michoacan, describes "a *tarima* placed on a water well to render the sound of a drum" (148).

Ochoa also explains how the *fandango* evolved into the *mariaches* (today's *mariachis*) and how it spread throughout the west, central Mexico and beyond the border "encouraged by the State and monopolized by those who controlled show business" (157). He emphasizes:

> In central and western Mexican lands, in its own way, with varying degrees of African kinship, each territory gave the *fandango* a singular touch that, according to circumstances and possibilities, encircled a universe of space, time, people, horses and other live stock, music, song, food, drink and gambling. (133)

Outside Veracruz, the *jarocho son* acquired new dimensions and gave birth to the *mariachi*. In addition to the lascivious *zapateado* and satirical *son* lyrics, the Veracruz or *jarocho* experience exported into the interior of the land forms of cooking and speech that in time interwove the fabric of Mexicaness. Reality persisted in popular culture despite monumental government efforts, instituted during the cultural phase of the Revolution, to "bleach out" the African presence from the national picture.

African Mexico can be observed in Mexican mestizo popular cultures: "While *La Bamba* is the most famous of the *sones jarochos*, there are somewhere around 100 others" (Carraher 1). A popular *mariachi son* is *El son de la negra* (The Black Woman's *Son*), *La Sandunga* is very popular as well. In Nayarit, the *jarabe* is formed by the *sones El Coamecate, El Diablo, Los Bules* and *Los Negritos*. These *sones* are called *potorricos*[28] "a dance where the man shows off his ability with the machete or with the knife" (Andrade 2).

African Mexican music, as its name implies, is a mestizo music generated by various previous cultural amalgamations. It is a hybrid of African, Amerindian, European and other ethnicities. What is certain is that the Mexican *son* is as African as anything else, and that this fact has been deliberately ignored notwithstanding its lyrics, rhythm, melody and harmony, which reveal to the common ear that Mexican music possesses a character that reaches beyond the Amerindian and Spanish experiences officially acknowledged as the sole parents of Mexican *mestizaje*.

The West African influence in the music of the Americas can be heard, seen and felt in Mexico's *jarocho* and *mariachi sones*. These musical traditions that engendered two of the most popular icons of Mexicaness: the *jarocho* dancers, and the *chinaco* and the *china*, are varieties of the Cuban *son*. The *son* complex spread all over the continent and was an element in much of the development of music. It may even have traveled back to Africa and Europe. Flamenco historians now accept the African American influence upon their dance (Sevilla 4), and anyone listening to the late Nigerian musician Fellah can discover the *salsa* flavoring his music.

A *fiesta*, *fandango* or *mariachi* without food is unthinkable. Just as in music, song and dance, Mexican culinary arts are the result of a complex amalgamation of *mestizajes*. Many of the foodstuffs and culinary techniques of today's Mexican cuisine came from other regions of the planet via the Spanish invasion. According to the *Cambridge World History of Food*, "In 1493 Columbus introduced horses, cattle, pigs, goats, and sheep to the New World." Also, according to the same source, "the gardens and orchards became much more diverse..." as a result of the encounter. The colonists brought cabbage, onions, carrots, lettuce, radishes, garlic, chickpeas, limes, lemons and sour oranges among others (Kiple 1279). But this complexity is not enough to handicap the senses and impair the perception of the African flavor and "know how" present along with the Amerindian and European components in national dishes such as *menudo* stew, famous in and out of Mexico.

Menudo is a derivative of the *mondongo* eaten all over the Americas, Spain and Portugal. By definition, *mondongo* refers to the innards of the animals. United States African Americans have a dish called "chitterlings" that is made with *mondongo* cooked in pinto beans with onion, garlic and spices. Argentinians cook *mondongo* with white corn, navy beans, chorizo, bacon and *zapallo criollo* (a type of squash) and call it *Locro Tucumano*. In Peru, it is said, "African slaves introduced the eating of animal entrails, as their owners didn't eat them. They invented *mondonguito*...." (Peruvian 1). In Venezuela, Colombia and Panama, *mondongo* is well known. In Costa Rica, at Limon's Carnival one can find *sopa de mondongo* (*La Nación* 1). Nicaragua's *mondongo* is a national dish advertised to attract tourists. Dominicans, Puerto Ricans and Haitians cook *mondongo* for many of their celebrations. In Yucatán, Mexico, there is a dish called *mondongo Kabic* (a dish said to have been introduced by Arabs) ("Museos" 2).

The United States Department of Health and Human services refers to *mondongo* stew in the "Afro-Hispanic" section of a study titled "Hispanics in the United States: An Insight into Group Characteristics." According to this study, "Spanish Caribbean was heavily affected by African grammatical patterns and loan words." *Mondongo* is identified as one of the "loan words" (Rodríguez 10).

All of this reveals a pattern: *mondongo* can be associated with the presence of black Africans. According to *Ethnologue*, in Zaire there is a village called *Mondongo* (Zaire 2). Aguirre Beltrán cites that the tribe *Mondonga* is "well known in Mexico and in other places of the Americas such as Haiti and the Danish island in the Antilles." He says that these people, among others, entered New Spain under the general name of "blacks from the Congo" (141).

Mexican *menudo* and *pancita* varieties are descendants of Veracruz *mondongo*. *Menudo* refers to entrails, although today the dish is generally cooked with beef tripe and hoofs only, hominy corn, peppers, garlic, and served with chopped onions, dry oregano and a wedge of lime (in some recipes tomatoes are used). Mexican *mondongo* is cooked with tripe including the part called fan and the *coágulo* (a dark inside stomach chamber), while *menudo* is usually cooked with *callo* (the outer part of the stomach) only; *mondongo* is cooked with *achiote* (annatto), tomatoes, onion, garlic, orange juice, and *epazote* (a Mexican herb). In central Mexico there are varieties of *mondongo* that are simply called *pancita* (small stomach).

Menudo stew is another recognized national icon of Mexicaness. It can be found as far as California, Chicago and New York and is associated with *mariachis* and with places where one would likely hear the word *chingar*. Is this association the result of the mass media image of the Mexican exported in the post-Revolution era, or is it the natural result of the cultural *mestizaje* (that extended throughout

Spanish territories that today are at least a third of the United States) whose roots are explored here? Either way, *menudo* is an internationally known Mexican dish that can be considered to have, among others, African roots like the famous maroon language of the people of Alvarado, Veracruz.

The people from Veracruz are nationally known for their *jarocho* celebrations. "Alvarado is one of the two towns (the other is Tlacotalpan), that have historically competed for recognition as the 'authentic' home of the *jarocho*" (González-El 173). Alvarado people are also nationally famous as *malhablados* (foulmouthed). They are known for the frequent use of the concept *chingar* in the most creative fashion. To hear two *Alvaradeños* arguing is to be in the presence of a living piece of the history of the *mestizaje* that Castilian underwent in Mexico, at least in part, due to the African influence.

Octavio Paz, in his renowned essay "Los hijos de la Malinche," explains that the word *chingar* is "a word heard only among men or in great parties" (70). He places it among the foul words, which he calls "the only living language in a world of anemic voices" (67). He sees it as a word in which an important part of the Mexican character is expressed, and explains its meaning in the light of the Conquest (77). For Paz, *chingar* is a word that speaks of Mexican history, a word that comes from the innermost part of Mexicaness. What he fails to recognize is that from the perspective of African Mexicans —the creators of the concept— *chingar* narrates the white led rape, pillage and plunder of Amerindians, Africans and Asians, among others, during the Spanish enterprise. *Chingar* is at the center of the occurrence; it brings back from memory and continues to narrate the image of subjugated women being taken by brutal force.

The word then, from *chingar* becomes *la chingada*, the raped woman. *La chingada* is also a metaphor for the subjugated nation. The conqueror becomes *El chingón*, the paternal figure of a supposed success, the mythical image of a warped greatness, the sick model to be emulated, prized and respected by all under him, including his bastard sons and daughters *los hijos de la chingada*. *Los hijos de la chingada* are literally the sons and daughters of the raped one: the *pelados, léperos, chinacos, teporochos, nacos, pitos*…the *mezclas* that by the end of the eighteenth century became the majority of the population in Mexico. The *hijos de la chingada*, the mestizos and the *mezclas* all are one, whose character makeup or ethnicity includes the African element.

Paz correctly states, "[t]he character of the Mexicans is the product of the social circumstances prevailing in our country [and that] the history of Mexico, which is the history of those circumstances, contains the answer to all questions" (64). However, Paz's perspective on the Mexican character lacks a crucial element: the black African participation, or the Africaness intrinsic to the character he analyzes.

In "*El verbo chingar: una palabra clave*" (The verb *chingar:* a key word), Rolando Antonio Pérez Fernández tracks the African legacy of the word. Contrary to all previous affirmations about the roots of the word *chingar*, including that of Octavio Paz in *El laberinto,* he finds that *chingar* is of Kimbundu origin, a language of the Bantu family. According to Pérez Fernández, *chingar* is a word bequeathed by Angolan slaves (307) whose presence and influence in Mexico as well as in all of the Americas is well established (Aguirre Beltrán 139, 141). Pérez Fernández' theory traces the word even to Brazil. He explains "the great influence Kimbundu has had in Brazilian Portuguese" given the previous close relations between Angola and Brazil (318).

In the Mexican context, this theory becomes plausible in light of the location of colonial *obrajes* (textile industry slave shops) legally restricted to Puebla, Michoacan, Guanajuato, Querétaro, Tlaxcala, Oaxaca and Mexico; that in the seventeenth century a good number of black slaves labored in that industry (Reynoso 23); and that there was continuous commercial contact with other parts of the Colony where the word *chingar*, or a derivative, is present.

The word *chingar* may be traced from Veracruz to practically all of Mexico and the Americas where the black African presence is an integral part of the making of nations and identities in addition to being an historical fact. *Chingar* can be found in the company of the *fandango* or "great parties," where the foul word called poetry by Paz, may be heard.

Moreover, according to the *Atlas cultural de México*, Mexican Spanish is a super-dialect divided into other dialects. These include the *altiplano meridional* dialect spoken in parts of Michoacan, parts of Guerrero, parts of Oaxaca and Morelos, Mexico City, the state of Mexico, parts of Tlaxcala, parts of Puebla and parts of Hidalgo (*Atlas* 167); and the word *chingar* is a major piece of the cultural heritage reflected by this dialect.

The *jarocho son*, the *mariachi*, the fandango, the *menudo* stew, and the voice *chingar*, are all national icons or emblems of Mexican cultural identity. They all have black African roots at the point of origin along with the Amerindian, Spanish, and other roots.

50

Notes

[1] Melgoza (170).

[2] According to Aguirre Beltrán, the first "Afro-Mestizos" received different names in the different regions of New Spain (169) and that "Jarocho was the name given in the region of Veracruz to the mix of black and Indian" (179).

[3] In 1995, it is reported that 88% of the total population speak Spanish and "8% speak Indian languages ... the number of languages listed for Mexico is 295. Of those, 289 are living languages and 6 are extinct." There are also 400, 000 people registered as "Arabic" and 31,000 as "Chinese" (Grimes 1).

[4] Néstor García Canclini uses the concept "hybrid cultures" in *Hybrid Cultures: Strategies for Entering and Leaving Modernity.* Trans. Christopher L. Chiappari and Silvia L. López. Minneapolis: U of Minnesota Press, 1995.

[5] A paraphrase made by Miguel Alberto Bartolomé in "Indians and African Mexicans at the end of the Century" from the words of the Brazilian Floristán Fernández (Bartolomé 300). It refers to a person who is oblivious of non-white people's plight against the white superiority syndrome.

[6] The intention of this work is to give credit to the African contribution to *mestizaje* without taking credit away from others.

[7] The comics studied as vehicles for mass persuasion under Richard Jackson's African Hispanic American optic would include *Memín Pingüín*, a Mexican publication (of a black single mother and her "devilish" son) of impressive circulation from the 50s to the present that contributed to caricaturing the African Mexican image.

[8] "*Jarocho 'son'* is a song and dance tradition that synthesizes African improvisation, poly-rhythm, and buck-board dancing with Native American dance patterns and Spanish *zapateado* footwork. Musicians play '*jarana*' (a type of guitar), '*pandero*' (tambourine), and '*arpa*' (harp) while dancers challenge one another. Rhythmic heel beats punctuate strummed melodies of songs whose lyrics tell of love and lust. People of coastal towns such as Alvarado and Tlacotalpan dance *jarocho* to celebrate almost every holiday or feast day" (González-El 139).

[9] According to Mario Pei, a dialect is a "specific form of a given language, spoken in a certain locality or geographic area, showing sufficient differences from the standard or literary form of that language, as to pronunciation, grammatical construction, and idiomatic usage of words, to be considered a distinct entity, yet not sufficiently distinct from other dialects of the language to be regarded as a different language" (56).

[10] A type of magazine developed from the comic format where photographs are used instead of illustrations.

[11] In the perspective adopted here, a symbol of popular culture ceases to be when it is absorbed by the homogenizing agents: for instance, the image of the *charro* (Jalisco cowboy) and the *china* is but a mass media bleached out image

of the original "*chinaco*" and "*china*" from Puebla.
[12] There were slaves from India and other Asian lands brought to Mexico as well (Aguirre Beltrán 148).
[13] This head is interesting when paired with the Brazilian information about the human fossil "Luiza" unveiled recently. They reopen the page for the investigation of pre-Colombian black people in the Americas. Luiza is a "woman's skull with features like an Australian aborigine" and is said to be 11,500 years old ("America's..."). The Olmec heads show features that have been ascribed to black Africans and are dated well before the recorded arrival of the Spanish and enslaved Africans to America.
[14] For an extensive account of "blood mixes" and percentages found in Mestizo-America see Claudio Esteva-Fabregat's *Mestizaje in Iberian-America* where he points out the existence of millions of "Blacks who appear white" in the United States alone, a window that allows a reasonable person to see the additional millions of this phenotype all over the Americas (Esteva 305). The north American Sinclair Lewis, the 1930 Nobel Prize winner, in his novel *Kingsbloodroyal* (1947) deals with the "white superiority syndrome" in the United States. According to Jackson this is a condition marked by "a fraudulent denial of an African heritage, though running the risk of discovery" (*The Black* 10). Francisco Arriví exposes this problem in Puerto Rico in his play, *Vejigantes* (1958); and the Mexican playwright, Celestino Gorostiza, analyzes it in a roundabout manner in *El color de nuestra piel* (1952); and Frantz Fanon diagnoses it in *Black Skin White Masks* (1952).
[15] "*Chino*" (Chinese) was the name given to Asian slaves, whether Chinese or not, brought through Acapulco in the yearly *Galeón de la China* (Galleon from China) without interruption until Independence (Aguirre Beltrán 49-52). The name "*china*" or "*chino*" was applied in the region of Puebla to the children of blacks and Indians. "In the seventeenth and eighteenth centuries to say mulatto or chino was the same (...) By the nineteenth century the name *chinaco* was given to the famous guerrilla fighters that fought against the French invasion" (Aguirre Beltrán 179). A good description of these African Mexican men and women can be found in Manuel Payno's *Los bandidos de Río Frío*. Moreover, in today's Mexico "*pelo chino*" designates curly hair.
[16] *Jarabe* has various meanings; here it describes a dance typical of many Hispanic American countries and of Mexico as well. One of the most typical Mexican *jarabes* today is the *jarabe tapatío*. But it is also important to consider other meanings of the word because in a *fandango* double and triple meanings apply. *Jarabe* is a sweet drink made from cooked sugar and fruit, or cooked sugar and plant, or herbal juices that may be used, given the case, as a refreshing or medicinal drink. A good fiesta, or a good song, or a good dance can be "refreshing" or "medicinal" as well as allowing the release of tensions. *Jarabe de pico* refers to a bunch of small talk. To give *jarabe* means to sweeten up a person.

52

[17] See Thomas Walker's "Hendrix in Black and White;" and *Mr. Rock and Roll: The Allan Freed Story.*

[18] Marvin A. Lewis in his *Afro-Argentine Discourse: Another Dimension of the Black Diaspora* cites: *El tema del tango en la literatura argentina* by Tomás Lara, Inés Leonilda and Ronetti de Panti; *Buenos Aires, negros y tango* by Oscar Natale; *La historia del tango: sus orígenes* by Manuel Pampin; and *La música y danza de los negros en el Buenos Aires de los siglos XVIII y XIX* by Ricardo Rodríguez Molas. Another interesting source is *El tango afrocubano, el tango andaluz, el tango criollo* by Norberto A. Bevilacqua.

[19] Yanga, during the late sixteen and early seventeen century was the "leader of a group of maroon, or run away slaves...in [Veracruz,] Mexico... [His group] became the only group of blacks in colonial Mexico to secure their freedom through rebellion and to have that freedom guaranteed by law..." (*Africana* 2034).

[20] It must be noted that in Mexico music and dancers without rhythm are referred to as "sin sabor" (without spice); that "Cuban music to be really good must have *sandunga,* a word combination probably made from "salt in Andalusian...and ndungdu, black African pepper" (Alén 9); and that in Venezuela the *contradanza,* besides referring to the French square dance, signifies a well-seasoned plate of black beans and white rice.

[21] Edward Said, in his introduction to *Culture and Imperialism,* points out that "stories are at the heart of what explorers and novelists say about strange regions of the world; they also become the method colonized people use to assert their own identity and the existence of their own history.... The power to narrate, or to block other narratives from forming and emerging, is very important to culture and imperialism, and constitutes one of the main connections between them" (xii-xiii). Said's words echo Jackson's differentiating between *positive* and *negative mestizaje.*

[22] It is widely documented that besides full contingents of African Mexican warriors, at least two of the major leaders of the freedom movement, José María Morelos y Pavón (Aguirre Beltrán 165) and Vicente Guerrero (Vincent 7), were African Mexicans.

[23] Pérez Monfort explains that according to the *Diccionario de autoridades* "[*fandango*] is a dance introduced in Spain by those who have been to the kingdoms of the Indies" probably at the end of the seventeenth century, and says that the same reference points out a possible Mandingo etymology of *fanda* "get-together" or "feed" and the pejorative *ango.* "Thus, fandango would be a 'fiesta where one eats', 'Fiesta to get together and enjoy' " (20).

[24] Professor Derek Carr, who specializes in Medieval and Golden Age Spanish Literature, mentioned the existence of the voice "*son*" prior to the time referred to here. He mentioned a voice *son* that comes from the Latin *sonus* "sound." The origins of the voice *son* as understood here are unknown to us, however it should be mentioned that there is a curious relation between the word "*songa*"

(irony, mockery) found in the Spanish dictionary and the way the *son* referred to here was used by non-whites to act out grievances and challenges to persons and the establishment itself.

[25] He is likely referring to the music derived from West African music that became African Antillean or African Caribbean music and then after its arrival on the continental land became African Amerindian Hispanic music. It must be stressed that there was interchange and exchange and that the Americas influenced Africa, Asia and Europe.

[26] In Mexico, a *palenque* is a place where the lower classes gathered to see cock fights, to have festivals or, as in the case here, to see a profane performance. It may be interesting to note also that *palenque* is the name given in Colombia to maroon (runaway slaves) villages such as *El Palenque de San Basilio*.

[27] Likely a relative of the African European American Tap Dance: an "art form indigenous to the United States that combines African and European dance with complicated jazz-based percussive sensibility created by elaborate foot work" (*Africana* 1826)

[28] An apparent corruption of "puertorricos" meaning from Puerto Rico: in the area of Michoacan, Colima and Nayarit there is a dance called *La danza de los viejitos* (The Little Old Men Dance) where people are dressed, mask and all, in the same manner as *Los Viejos* (The Old Men) in Puerto Rico's African Boricua Festival of *Santiago Apostol* in Loíza (Cepeda 15).

Three

La vida inútil de Pito Pérez: Tracking the African Contribution to the Mexican Picaresque Sense of Humor

> We are dealing with an important sector of Mexican anonymous society whose African ancestors arrived on request through a controlled black market. Heirs who, ripped from their cherished and scarcely known far-off mother, somehow stamped a deep imprint in the lineage and culture of the Mexican West, in Jal-Mich and in the North-West of the same Michoacan entity.
> Álvaro Ochoa Serrano

> Blacks may lose their form, but they never lose their essence.
> Rafael Murillo-Selva Rendón[1]

As seen in the two prior chapters, Mexican *mestizaje* implicated people from all corners of the world. The three main branches of this amalgamation come from pre-Columbian American indigenous peoples, peoples from a four hundred kilometer strip of Western black Africa, and from the no less diverse and colorful Spaniards,[2] among other ethnicities. The Africaness of Mexican *mestizaje* is often denied or unknown in Mexico and abroad. As mentioned in Chapter One, until recently Mexicaness has been attributed to the mix between Spaniards and Amerindians.

This is starting to change. At the academic level it is now accepted that Mexican *mestizaje* has a black African "third root." One of the problems with this Eurocentric perspective is that while an African presence is acknowledged, it is understood as a thing of the past. Another reason for the subordination of Africa and the elevation of Spain is that as far as Mexican (mestizo) "culture" is concerned, the prevailing understanding is that the cultural texts that emerged from the colonial experience are in Spanish.

This is like saying that all music played on a guitar is Arabic because the instrument is originally Arabic. Spanish has been an instrument for expressing experiences and the feelings born from them. The Africaness that literally blossomed in the new environment is imbedded in the rhythm of the *sones* and in the new musicality Mexican Spanish acquired through concepts such as *chingar*. Devoid of its Africaness, it is impossible to comprehend Mexicaness.

Mexican Africaness can be verified with the senses: it can be seen, heard, touched, and tasted all over the land. Wherever one goes in Mexico and where Mexican mestizos are, characteristics that manifest Africa's ongoing participation in the construction of the modern nation are obvious. In popular Mexico, one can appreciate the indelible African branding (stronger than the Spanish hot iron and the *criollo* myths) that pierced its way to the very soul of the country. This is confirmed by popular Mexican worldviews, food, music, language, and sense of humor.

La vida inútil de Pito Pérez (1938) by José Rubén Romero (1890-1952), from this perspective, acquires an additional dimension, particularly when considering the origins of the Mexican rogue, *mezcla*, *lépero*, or *pícaro* which will be sketched following a brief revisiting of the critical approach informing this study, and the introduction of the novel's structure, plot and genre.

La vida inútil is a staunch critique of the government, its institutions, the clergy, and the *criollo* elite. It is a mockery and condemnation of common people, who according to the central character, *Pito Pérez*,[3] remain enslaved by their beliefs and inertia (183). *La vida* is a testament of contempt toward a destiny that allows Mexican *Pito Pérezes* to develop a warped sense of love, a total desire—plagued with eroticism—for death itself. However, and beyond this, the novel, although in a hard-to-perceive fashion, is informed by a white aesthetic.

Jackson has found that black phobia and a white aesthetic pervades a considerable part of Latin American literature that refers to blacks and their descendants. Beauty, morality, civility, gallantry, bravery, prowess, industriousness, restraint, sincerity, intellectuality, good-heartedness, and love-for-life, among other virtues, are measured according to the amount of whiteness a person appears to have; in short, the closer to white the better. This worldview repeats and reinforces stereotypes of non-white people. Once it is placed in the channels of persuasion and reaches the masses it develops into codes that actually warp memory and identity, thus the perception of self.

La vida inútil, according to the central character and narrator, *Pito Pérez,* is a mind twister, a psychoanalytical novel (125). It is a novel wherein the reader is introduced to the psychology of a drunkard[4] who observes the situation of his time and place, the first decades of twentieth century Mexico while the modern nation is being born.

What happened after the civil war known as "the Mexican Revolution"? What happened to the institutions? What happened to the masses? Who made up the masses? What was life like in Michoacan (the setting of *Pito*'s story) during the first four decades of the century? How did people feel in general? What did they eat? What else had been achieved beyond the killing of nearly ten percent of the national population (about a million), the majority of which were socially non-white people? On what basis was the modern nation narrated?

A full response to these questions is beyond the parameters of this chapter. Nevertheless, a reading inclusive of a partial reply to the problem is feasible, particularly in the light of Brushwood where he expresses:

> The novel is capable of expressing the reality of a nation given its ability to cover both visible reality and the elements that are not seen. In its pinnacle the novel explores internal reality, which is a deeper part of the existing circumstance and also the dreams that transcend what is visible in a different direction. It is capable of inquiring in both directions about the visible circumstances without toning down its conscience or the reader's conscience. (Preface ix)

La vida inútil was published in 1938. It has been made into black and white and color films; it has been adapted for the theater and performed a number of times. It was translated into English in 1966. It has been taught in many United States universities since that time and made into video documentaries. Articles and criticism of the novel exist by the dozens in prestigious publications. Five thousand copies of the seventeenth Spanish language edition of the novel appeared in 1970. By 1995, it had been printed thirty-six times. The thirty-sixth edition, the edition used here, was of ten thousand copies. The novel has 232 pages divided into three sections. The first two sections are numbered I, and II and the third section is titled "Some of *Pito Perez's* things left in the inkwell." The first part is divided into eight chapters without number, each of which is an anecdote of *Pito*'s non-love affairs. The second part is divided into four additional unnumbered chapters as well, where other circumstances of *Pito*'s existence are narrated. The third and last section, written as a post-statement, is divided into five numbered chapters.

The first part of the novel, referring to something that happened before 1910 when the armed phase of the Mexican Revolution started, is a series of stories about *Pito*'s life and his contacts with people. They are tales from memory painted on bucolic landscapes; roguish tales told by a drunkard from the bell tower of his native town's church. They are ghoulish anecdotes told to the narrator (*Pito*'s neighbor, a poet in the making). This is done right before *Pito* abruptly abandons Santa Clara del Cobre (38).

This first section imparts that *Pito*'s has a bitter perception of life and is excessively suffering (12). The reader learns that *Pito* prefers autochthonous products: food (13), people (21), and national drinks (21). The reader becomes aware of *Pito*'s love for truth and his hatred toward the elites (15) and "the compendium of a whole social world, crammed with injustice and inequality" (15), a world where the people in control prefer what is European (21). *Pito* sketches the state of a few institutions before 1910 when the armed conflict began. He narrates his childhood and analyzes the circumstances that made him appear as a true madman (16) and which isolated him socially, such as a paradoxical "theft" of the church's moneybox while he was an altar boy (26-34).

The second part of the novel is formed by another series of anecdotes about *Pito*'s life. The narrator runs again into *Pito* by chance in Morelia, the capital city of Michoacan ten years later (after 1920 when the armed phase of the revolution had officially ended). This part of the narrative describes a crude social reality that would seem more like fiction (169). *Pito* is underemployed, selling odds and ends. When the narrator reproaches him for leaving without saying good-by, *Pito* replies that he had to go "to keep on living and thus have something to say" (147). Also, by way of an hallucination suffered by *Pito*, religious beliefs are questioned by exposing that even in heaven there are social differences due to skin color (173). *Pito's* romantic affair with death, *la Caneca,* is disclosed (175) and *Pito* is found dead "on a heap of trash, his hair messy, and full of mud. His mouth contracted by a bitter grin and his eyes sourly staring toward heaven with a daring look" (181).

In the third part, some anecdotes on *Pito*'s life are told after his death. This section is an ode to *Pito*'s unfortunate life and is utilized to finish developing the central character, a *pelado, mezcla* or *lépero* prototype, and to describe a time and place under siege by foreign people and their interests. What cannot be said about a dead tramp? The narrator expounds in an elegy:

> There are knaves for whom everything turns out fine due to good luck, and unfortunate rogues, such as our friend Jesús Pérez Gaona [*Pito*'s Christian name], who never told a lie and whose word nobody believed in; who never killed even an insect and from whom everyone ran as though running from a murderer; who ingeniously found food yet stayed a beggar; one who searched for the comfort of love and found general contempt and indifference from all women to the point of stating ironically: my hand will be my very widow? (190)

This last part of the novel points out that *Pito* was never a friend to civil or ecclesiastical authority because both offer punishment in this life as well as in the afterlife, and neither one "offered him a piece of bread" (210).

La vida is a story of the unequal struggle between a Mexican commoner and his late nineteenth century and early twentieth century circumstance. *Pito* and society are the main actors. Secondary characters serve as background and come to life only as community. No one is forged as an individual; rather they are presented as a mass of characteristics.

As a smith forging a piece, the author creates recognizable images out of the anonymous mass. Romero gives form, life, and color to a part of the people erased through the ideology of *mestizaje.* Romero seems to laugh at himself and makes us laugh at ourselves while drinking and making us drink slowly the bitter contents of the calyx of truth, a reality that sip-by-sip burns all the way to the soul. Sparks fly out from his hammer while he makes popular poetry, the very satire coming from the spirit of a people whose unwanted image is not reflected in the nation's mirror; a people capable of laughing to tears, notwithstanding the paradox of "existing" and not seeing themselves reflected, due to a sense of humor developed by forever walking hand in hand with Death itself. A people, former slaves, who as a part of daily life withstood the stench of freely abused flesh; a people who have relentlessly fought an unequal fight, to be able to die with dignity at least. The internal conflict of the Mexican does not come from the conflict between two roots nor from her/his incapacity to reconcile three, it is the result of the incomprehensible human experience she/he has lived.

La vida inútil de Pito Pérez echoes the anonymous *La Vida de Lazarillo de Tormes y de sus fortunas y adversidades* (1554) (*Lazarillo de Tormes' Life: his Fortunes and Adversities*), "A book surrounded by mystery that continues to pose three enigmas: author, date it was written, and meaning of the story" (Aguirre Belver 13). *La vida de Lazarillo* is considered one of the most important prose works in the Spanish language.   It describes the experiences of a rogue who runs into hunger and misery when he engages work as a blind person's guide, as an altar boy, and as a servant to a squire. In doing so, he develops a scathing view of life and the circumstances surrounding him. *La vida de Lazarillo* describes the society of his day. This novel is considered among one of the first picaresque novels in Castilian Spanish.[5]

La vida inútil is nothing new regarding its genre. Nonetheless, at least two fundamental points make it different from *La vida de Lazarillo*: in *La vida inútil*, the author is known, and it introduces a sense of humor that possesses new colors.

La vida inútil informs the reader that the author is the narrator (187), and that it is he who judges society due to *Pito*'s death, or unfortunate life, when he expresses, "misery does not breed happiness, and poor people's laughter, when they laugh day in and day out, seems to be a grimace of pain" (189).

The sense of humor reflected in *La vida inútil* is mainly a product of: the experience of Amerindian people; people from black Africa; "certain Hispanic popular expressions" (Pérez Monfort 17); and the result of the amalgamation of all and every one of them. The sense of humor in *La vida inútil* is far from being a simple Spanish transplant. Hispanic popular culture[6] plays an instrumental role. However, the sense of humor acquires additional dimensions in the light of the Transatlantic Slave Trade, and the subjugation and enslavement of black, Amerindian, and Asian people, among others. It informs the reader that the sense of humor therein is a product of the Mexican experience of which the black experience, so adamantly denied, is nevertheless a major player. The present chapter will take this premise as its point of departure.

Pablo González Casanova identifies the first profane dances and songs (*sones, jarabes* etc.) as the roots of Mexican popular satire (82). These songs and dances are singular not only because they were persecuted by the Inquisition, but because "they are the most audacious mockery of religion and death, because they never abandon the delight of evoking sexual passes, and because, saving few occasions, they are related to holy things" (González Casanova 65). From within this satire, according to González Casanova, "customs, ceremonies, education, authorities, prayer, death and even God, acquire a new meaning" (87).

As a consequence of the controversy between the anonymous rogues or *pícaros* and the Church, criticism of the system matures during the eighteenth century and a "vigorous political conscience is acquired" (González Casanova 97). From here, a public opinion is born that, beyond addressing personal differences, establishes relations between people and institutions, and institutions and the state, to become a public critical stance with a political reach which foreshadows the arrival of the Independence movement in the beginning of the nineteenth century and that by 1810 will climax with the onset of the political severance of New Spain from Spain.

The independent journalist, José Joaquín Fernández de Lizardi (1776-1827), is perhaps the best-known writer of satirical fliers until the late 1820's. As a critic of the political and social environment inherited from the colonial period, he wrote under the pen name *El pensador mexicano* (The Mexican Thinker). He initiated the novelistic tradition in Mexico (and perhaps in Latin America as well). Fernández de Lizardi may have been the first to write an antislavery novel in the New World.[7]

In 1816, Fernández de Lizardi published *El periquillo sarniento (The Mangy Parrot)*, a work that follows the Spanish picaresque structure. However, *El periquillo* differs as it denounces inhumanity, cruelty, and the irrationality of slavery (726-35). Therefore, it takes the genre to dimensions unknown by its predecessors. Carmen Ruiz Barrionuevo points out "Lizardi took advantage of a picaresque mold inherited from Spanish and Hispanic-American experiences and shaped it to serve his purpose and thereby made it apt for new heights" (Fernández [*Introducción*] 40).

The debate continues as to whether *El periquillo* is a picaresque work, implying that if it were picaresque, the work would lack originality. At this juncture the same problem is faced by *La vida inútil* written over a hundred years later. A full response is outside the parameters of this chapter. Nevertheless, it can be proposed that both novels reflect, in part, the worldviews of the vanquished Amerindians, and the black experience, and that both are written for social purposes, or in Ruíz Barrionuevo's words: "to confront pain, errors, and failure" (Fernández, Introduction 40).

From the perspective of this study, both novels are creative and do not lack originality. In the case of *El periquillo,* the voice is ready to part from colonial ideology. In *La vida inútil,* nineteenth-century ideology, at least in part, comes under attack. Both authors use Spanish language and picaresque structures as a vehicle, but they adapt it and give it new breadth in order to express a reality that, beyond being a Spanish extension, possesses its own dimensions.

Aguirre Beltrán discloses that the *mezclas,* "an inter-*casta* whose situation could not be more miserable" (173), were a mass of beings which, given an inept legislation and an unjust economy, could be found wandering all over the country and the cities, forced to resort to their wits to extract the bare minimum for survival. He points out that the number of drifters, "plebeians in the capital cities, shifters in the haciendas," grew to such an extent, and their lifestyle chipped into New Spain's economy to the point of provoking "slavery's decadence as it turned production based on slave-work unprofitable: the population of *mezclas* had grown to such a considerable size" (173).

Mezclas have been characterized under various derogatory names. They are known as: *léperos, pelados, teporochos, vagos, plebe, nacos, mugrosos,* among many others. They have received names according to historical need; a good example of this is *"chinaco."* Paradoxically, all of this name-calling is what allows the tracing of the *pícaro's* lineage and the making of the needed connections to inform this reading further. Payno, as mentioned in Chapter Two, described a collective character he observed within the city of Puebla during the representation of a profane colloquium in the central *palenque* in 1843. Payno divides the crowd he is observing into "two social oddities" (75). Part is comprised by *léperos* and the other by "beautiful *chinitas*" (73).

According to Aguirre Beltrán, in Puebla, the name *china* was given to the offspring of Amerindians and blacks during the seventeenth and eighteenth centuries and by the nineteenth century "*china, lépera* or prostitute connoted the same" thing (179).

Payno explains that the *lépero*'s existence is singular; notwithstanding all the country's cultural changes, it has been preserved intact (75). According to Payno, the *lépero* is the son of artisan fathers and house-servant mothers and usually lives in idleness. He says that although the *lépero* is not hard working in school, he is astute in worldly matters; and that, as there is no one to take care of him at home, he spends his life in the streets throwing stones, rolling around in the mud along with other children or pulling on a kite. "Normally, parents are unusually cruel when they correct minor faults, while they tolerate serious ones such as obscene language, and the small thefts he commits in the vicinity" (75).

In Payno's appraisal, the vagrants of centuries past are now underemployed and their children have inherited some characteristics such as *lépero* speech,[8] vagrancy, inclination for the worldly, and a challenging attitude toward the establishment, and particularly against the main censor of the time, the Catholic Church. This *lépero,* after turning into a temporary hero by fiercely fighting the better-equipped enemy forces during the French invasion, according to Aguirre Beltrán, acquires the name *chinaco* (179), the same name given to liberal soldiers during the War of Reform. These two "oddities" observed and described by Manuel Payno, that is, the *lépero* turned *chinaco,* and the *china*, became an icon of popular nationalism during the cultural phase of the Revolution, but not before erasing all traces of the African contribution to its formation.

The stories told in *La vida inútil* are from before 1910 and from right up to 1920. It is possible that the author wanted to provide an overview of the situation that ultimately triggered the armed conflict, and the conditions in the area left by the ten-year struggle. "There have been many yesterdays since we've seen one another! It's going to be ten years since the tower in Santa Clara" (147). Later the Revolution is recalled: "I have gone through battle-fields filled with corpses like a victorious general inhaling the stench of putrefied flesh" (157). Finally, the reader is taken to the days after the armed phase of the war when the narrator unexpectedly runs into *Pito* in Morelia (146).

La vida inútil records *Pito*'s "pilgrimage" throughout Michoacan (149) and the nearby area. Ochoa Serrano mentions that, according to Ramón Sanchez in 1896, the presence of visibly black Mexicans could be observed in various areas of the state (where *Pito* drifts in and out), for instance in the Jiquilpan district (93).

It is precisely in a Jiquilpan arcade that *Pito* goes to eat *menudo* (124), a stew offspring of the *mondongo* dish studied in Chapter Two. But the *menudo* is only one of the clues to unearth the African element present in the ethos and in the features of some of the characters in *La vida inútil*. Throughout the narrative, there are other keys and "psycho-alcoholic" digressions (221) that, although blurred and diluted, point toward the African dimension of the area where the anecdotes that divide this work take place.

Among the keys that point out the African element in the area's *mezclas* are the inference that *Pito* does not belong to the "privileged *castas*" (15); and that *Pito* is a *lépero* prototype, identified as a knave (21), who mocks modernity (28), who laughs at humanist precepts (183), who satirizes the clergy (210) and the privileged *castas* (58) and scorns the government (59, 82, 85), thus echoing his daring African ancestors who would gather in the plazas to drink spirits, sing profanities and dance lasciviously openly challenging the Catholic Church and the State. Another key is that *Pito* is a musician who plays the latest songs (36), popular themes (123), and that he is a people's poet (111, 113, 123-124, 178) whose mouth allows their "spirit to talk" (41).

Other signs in support of this reading are the "blackish" and "pockmarked" face of a priest whom *Pito* treats well, and whose mother and sister live in Santa Clara (62). It is also pointed out that Irene's skin is the "color of a cinnamon stick," that she is the daughter of a muleteer (92), and that the store belonging to *Pito*'s uncle is called *El Moro Musa* (97) (The Moor). This uncle's daughters, according to the narrator, would seem to be from different parents because they are "tall and blond and short and black" (97). Chucha, "the darkest in color" of the two daughters looks like a "naughty little monkey" (97), and she has "the white teeth of an unconscious little monkey" (103).

At the same time, other cultural texts are invoked when *los sones de la sierra y el jarabe* (110) and the dances popularly known as *las danzas bullangueras* (150) are mentioned. Moreover, direct references are made to the color line dividing poverty and the other side (173); in addition, "black" and "white" feminine "flesh" is brought into the picture to eroticize it, thus making it more attractive to the common person (200). A "blackish woman" is mentioned as well (203).

With all of these pieces of the picture it would be difficult to argue that the Mexican *lépero* prototype and his people presented in the novel are other than the historical Mexican *mezclas* in Michoacan area at the end of the nineteenth century and the beginning of the twentieth century. The image can be complemented with the following facts: in the district of Jiquilpan a noticeable African presence is documented at the end of the nineteenth century; and in the following places around Michoacan the black presence is recorded: Zamora, around the Chapala swamp (northeast Michoacan today), in Apatzingán, Pizándaro, Tacámbaro, Taretán, La Huacana, Tuzantla, Tancítaro, Valladolid (today Morelia, the capital city), Tlalpujahua, Ucareo-Tziritzícuaro, Zinapécuaro, Maravatío, Tuxpan, Taximaroa, Zitácuaro, Patzcuaro, Paracho, Ario, Turicato, Urecho, Apatzingán, Sirándaro, Zacatula, Peribán, Tlazazalca-La Piedad, Zamora-Jacona (Ochoa 73). Other places in the state can be mentioned, such as sugar mills, *haciendas* (farms or plantations), *obrajes* (rudimentary factories for manufacturing different goods), mines, and domestic jobs, where blacks were first utilized and their descendants, the *mezclas*, later.

The Michoacan "picaresque world"[9] evoked in *La vida inútil* informs the reader about the black presence and its influence in the area. This is confirmed by the popular taste for *los sones de la sierra* music, which echoes *los sones jarochos* and by extension the African-Cuban *sones montunos*. At the same time, this musical presence echoes the *mezcla* dances and songs persecuted during the colonial period, which are the basis of the Mexican satire (González Casanova 82). These dances and songs transmit the African taste and an African sense of humor. Under the idea of positive *mestizaje* that that is African in the Mexican mestizo and Mexican *mestizaje* is **African** and alive, and is significant to Mexicaness.

It is possible that the author of *La vida inútil* preferred the picaresque structure to address an extremely delicate topic: the state of the nation immediately before and after the Revolution from a point of view that at least superficially appears to be that of the man in the street. But what is revealed beyond the false tears[10] is a narrative skillfully woven in popular language that nevertheless propagates the "cosmic race" notions contained in the discourse on nation during the cultural phase of the Mexican Revolution.   Through a nearly seamless *criollo* adaptation of the *lépero* language and sense of humor, the author is able to take his message to the masses. His ventriloquism becomes evident, as the white aesthetic and black phobia informing his views are

detected under Jackson's lens. Jackson has identified the white
aesthetic as a pattern in other Latin American literary works produced
where there is—or there has been an African presence. Under the
white aesthetic and black phobia, a person, including non-whites,
actually comes to believe that only white is beautiful and sees as
inferior and ugly anything considered non-white. [11]

The white aesthetic is found to be present in *La vida inútil*
notwithstanding the explanation of the author where he points out that
Pito "was not a sensuous person obsessed neither with black nor with
white flesh" (200). During a delirious episode, *Pito* describes beauty as
"snow white shoulders" in a desired woman (168). When he refers to
Chucha, his cousin, after mentioning that she is the "more toasted in
color" and that her white teeth contrast with her color, he compares her
repeatedly with an "unconscious and naughty little monkey" (97, 102).
But this is not all. Father Pureco, described as having a "blackish and
pockmarked face," according to *Pito* is ignorant, intellectually
incapable, and naturally good (62-73). Also, a *son* musician is marked
by his speech form and his rhythm "I am tuned fo' *jarabe*" (110).

As a conclusion, a brief analysis of such descriptions in Jackson's
light will point out that non-white images in *La vida inútil* are
stereotypical and far from real. Departing from the stereotypes of
visibly black mestizos, a narrative responding to the *criollo* worldview
is found. Under this perspective, racial prejudice is maximized against
those people who deviate the most from the norm. The greatest beauty
is compared with "snow" yet the musician "cannot talk well" (he
swallows phonemes, thus echoing *jarocho* speech). "The acceptance of
these aesthetic standards produces those practices common in Latin
America ...by which individuals seek to 'whiten' themselves" (Jackson,
The Black xii). These are the type of stereotypical images that support
the myth of white beauty and the phobia against blacks and that
highlight the manner in which the white aesthetic has "taken a strong
foothold in the consciousness of Latin Americans of all colors
(Jackson, *The Black* xiii). Jackson explains:

> It has become clearer that the somatic distance, conditioned by
> archetypical images of color and corresponding racial myths, has had an
> enormous impact on the pattern of race relations in Latin America [...].
> The association of the color black with ugliness, sin, darkness, immorality,
> Manichean metaphor, with the inferior, the archetype of the lowest order,
> and the color white with the opposite of these qualities partly explains the
> racist preconceptions and negative images of the black man projected—at

times despite the author's good intentions—in much of [Latin American literature]. (*The Black* xiii)

Various authors cited by Jackson have made clear that racial stereotypes, prejudiced expressions, and racial terms, among others, are commonplace in Latin American literature and other American literatures:

> Racism and the white aesthetic exist in Spanish America, as in Brazil and the non-Hispanic Caribbean, as controlling factors in the lives of black people. Indeed, a cult of whiteness and a corresponding fear of blackness, whether ethnic, political, or social, are part of a tradition dramatized in Hispanic literature from Lope de Rueda's Eufemia (1576) to Francisco Arrivi's *Máscara puertorriqueña* (1971) with numerous examples to be found in between and after. (*The Black* xiv)

The white aesthetic, according to Jackson, beyond producing revealing instances of a white racial consciousness heritage, distorts the literary black image. In this type of narrative the black character does not go beyond being "purely and simply the sum of prejudices, myths, and collective attitudes of a given group" (*The Black* xiv). This, under James Snead's coding, sheds additional light on the topic of this study by bringing to the forefront the added negative effects toward blacks created by repeating and reinforcing stereotypes, something that *La vida inútil* certainly achieves and thereby becomes part of the discourse on nation developed by *criollos* in order to usurp power and keep it for themselves.

Notes

[1] Quoted from an interview of Rafael Murillo-Selva Rendón by Colombia Truque Vélez (Truque 36).

[2] It must be remembered that Spanish people in Europe commonly are considered "southerners" and more in line with Eastern Europeans, but not as "pure" and "advanced" as Nordic peoples.

[3] *Pito* in the *lépero* dialect means penis. Pérez is an extremely common name.

[4] The thesis of the drunkard-*pelado* here echoes the Mexican *pelado* thesis advanced a few years before by Samuel Ramos in *El perfil del hombre y la cultura de México* (*The Profile of Man and Culture in Mexico*) (1934)—where

68

the *pelado or lépero* is a pathetic and worthless being, an extra load impeding modernization.

[5] The other picaresque novel considered among the first in Castilian Spanish is *Guzmán de Alfarache: Vida y hechos del pícaro* (1599-1604) by Mateo Alemán.

[6] Antonio García de León explains, "Generally, when one mentions the baroque in its various manifestations, one forgets the circularity and interdependence existing between popular culture and written academic culture, particularly, in the almost intangible territory of literature and music (García de León 111).

[7] According to Salvador Bueno in "El negro en *El Periquillo Sarniento*: antirracismo de Lizardi."

[8] *Jarocho* speech, the one from Tlacotalpan and Alvarado, Veracruz, is well known in Mexico as *lépero* speech. It must be remembered that the name "*jarocho* was the term applied in Veracruz to the offspring of black and Amerindian" (Aguirre 179).

[9] Fernando O Assunção, in *El tango y sus circunstancias*, uses the concept *mundo picaresco* (picaresque world) to define a time and place in the middle of the nineteenth-century Rio de la Plata area during the genesis of the Tango dance, songs and worldview. Among other experiences, Tango is linked to the black experience in the South American zone (23-85).

[10] Jackson introduces the concept "False Tears for the Black Man" in *The Black Image in Latin American Literature* (Contents vii).

[11] Gorostiza's drama from the "Identity Theatre" *El color de nuestra piel* (*The Color of Our Skin*) (1952) puts an end to the myth that Mexico is a racial democracy (Neglia 164). Through a psychological analysis of a Mexican mestizo family, where there is a blond and blue eyed son along with a darker brother and sister and a father who denies being a mestizo himself though he is light dark, Gorostiza confronts his audience with the fact that well after four hundred years of intermixing, Mexican mestizos, fair and dark, continue to be non-white and the practitioners of what Quince Duncan has called "racist psychocide" (53). Two syndromes may describe this condition, a legacy of Vasconcelos' ideology, and its current effect on non-white Mexicans: the "white superiority syndrome" marked by a "fraudulent denial of an African heritage, though running the risk of discovery" (Jackson, *The Black* 10); and the false memory syndrome where the subjects affected have been persuaded that something that exists never was.

Four

Angelitos negros, a Film from the "Golden Age"[1] of
Mexican Cinema: Coding Visibly Black Mestizos By
and Through a Far-reaching Medium

> The coding of blacks in film, as in the wider society, involves a history of
> images and signs associating black skin color with servile behavior and
> marginal status.   While these depictions may have reflected prior
> economic oppression of blacks, they also tend to perpetuate it. Through
> the exact repetition which is film's main virtue, these associations became
> part of film's typological vocabulary..."Codes" are not singular portrayals
> of one thing or another, but larger, complex relationships.
>
> James Snead

The family melodrama, *Angelitos negros* (1948) (*Little Black
Angels*), produced in Mexico by the Rodríguez Brothers and directed
by Joselito Rodríguez, is a cinematographic message[2] about visibly
black Mestizos broadcasted by a far-reaching medium.[3]   This black-
and-white sound motion picture is a graphic example of the
homogenizing discourse on nation adopted and institutionalized by the
Partido Revolucionario Institucional (PRI) (Institutional Revolutionary
Party) during the cultural phase of the Mexican Revolution (1920-
1968).   It is part of the ethnic integration or whitening discourse of that
period, found in Mexican film,[4] literature, music, dance, painting, and
images, which were made standard credentials of national identity.

Angelitos negros is a salient illustration of a pervasive Eurocentric way of thinking that engendered the myth of a "cosmic race" as the modern nation was being built. This myth was used to obliterate from national memory and identity the Africaness of *mestizaje* while claiming that Africans and their descendents had been "diluted," "assimilated" or "integrated" to disappearance.

Angelitos negros is the story of the "suffering" and "misfortunes" of Ana Luisa, a racist, well-off, educated visibly blond woman. Ana Luisa does not know, until the story begins to unfold, that she is the daughter of "Mercé" (Mercedes), her visibly black housemaid and that therefore Africa runs in her veins. As the story develops, Mercé confesses to the catholic priest that Ana Luisa de la Fuente is her daughter:

> I was the maid in the house owned by her father, Don Agustín de la Fuente. He was a rich widower. She was born *white* as him, *blond* as the sun. She was so beautiful he began to love her. He decided to give her his name and his fortune so long as I did not claim her. What mother in my place would not have accepted? It was a matter of my daughter's happiness. He was such a good man that he allowed me to stay to take care of her. When he died we were left alone. She doesn't know anything about this. She must never find out. (*Angelitos*)

Ana Luisa marries a white-looking mestizo orphan, José Carlos Ruiz, a famous singer who refers to himself, and is referred to by Mercé, as "white." Superficially, José Carlos is kind to all visibly black people and apparently he is free from racial prejudice. When Ana Luisa and José Carlos have Belén, a mulatto daughter, the conflict erupts.

As the melodrama continues, José Carlos learns from Mercé that Ana Luisa is her daughter but agrees not to reveal Mercé's life secret because this knowledge, according to the catholic priest's advice, may be life-threatening for Ana Luisa's already frail emotional state (caused by her giving birth to visibly black Belén). However, when Ana Luisa strikes Mercé, causing her to fall down the stairs, José Carlos can no longer keep silent and suddenly reveals to Ana Luisa that Mercé is her mother. Ana Luisa had thought that her daughter's blackness came from José Carlos' bloodline. From the time of Belen's birth, she had gone into a deep depression for what she saw as her greatest misfortune (having a black child) and made José Carlos' life and everybody else's life miserable.

In the end, Ana Luisa comes to her senses after causing her mother's death by injury. Then she appears to come to terms with her "fate." Following this, José Carlos readily absolves Ana Luisa: from having abused her mother to death; from having abused her child by openly and publicly rejecting and denying any relation to her for years; from having publicly discriminated against his visibly black friends; from having abused him directly over the years when Ana Luisa accused him of destroying her life by giving her a black child. The storyline echoes the fallacy that Mexico is some sort of a racial democracy and that there is no black resistance.

Following a brief historical preamble on Mexican cinema to set the context for the argument, this chapter will analyze the manner in which stereotypes of black people are used to code visibly black Mexicans in *Angelitos negros* in order to propagate and perpetuate the idea that blacks are inferior.[5] This chapter proposes that the message regarding black people in *Angelitos negros* is a reproduction, adapted for Spanish speaking audiences, of *Imitation of Life* (1934) a Hollywood[6] film directed by John Stahal and Claudine Colbert. It explains how a white supremacy message moves through languages and cultures promoting images that are more fantastic than real. It demonstrates that the message in *Angelitos negros* deploys a Eurocentric mass-produced negative view of black people for mass consumption and that the predominant aesthetic of *Angelitos negros* is the white aesthetic.

James Snead's approach in *White Screens Black Images: The Dark Side of Hollywood* (1994) is incorporated into Jackson's perspective. This enables an aesthetic "reading" of the characterization and portrayal of black people in *Angelitos negros* in terms of the codes reproduced and reinforced through the stereotypical images of black people in the film (Snead 136). Snead states:

> Stereotypes ultimately connect to form larger complexes of symbols and connotations. These codes then begin to form a kind of "private conversation" among themselves without needing to refer back to the real world for their facticity. The pleasure of recognizing codes displaces the necessity for a viewer to verify them. Since many mass-media images today claim to be neither reality nor fantasy (witness the docu-drama), there are no useful criteria by which to inspect or challenge the claims to truth that these visual images and events constantly make. (141)

Ella Shohat and Robert Stam, in *Unthinking Eurocentrism: Multiculturalism and the Media*, bring to the forefront of the debate on stereotyping in popular culture some methodological questions "about the underlying premises of character or stereotype-centered approaches" (198). They warn that, "the exclusive preoccupation with images, whether positive or negative, can lead to a kind of essentialism" (199). Shohat and Stam bring to light the complexity of the question through a series of examples of what they see as a "black experience." They propose that that experience differs according to the various cultural contexts where it occurs. Shohat and Stam conclude that a critique of stereotyping should begin only after a film has been understood within its cultural milieu and not "as the application of an *a priori schema*" (213).

While a work should be analyzed within its cultural context, it should be clear as well that any expressed mode of thinking or discourse dealing with the question of blacks of the *Maafa* or black holocaust, including *Angelitos negros*, needs to be concurrently understood within a worldwide context to avoid the possibility of regionalizing, reducing, or minimizing a truly universal problem that has affected for centuries and continues to affect people across cultures and languages at a global level.

This approach is relevant here because a narrative form that carries an adverse message first conceived in another language and culture is at issue. The message was developed in the United States. So, did Hollywood export messages based on its world-view, that is, on the manner in which it perceived blacks? Was this world-view acceptable and adaptable across languages and cultures for the reproduction and reinforcement of an adverse discourse on blacks at a continental (or world) level?

Although the script of *Angelitos negros* is solely attributed to Joselito Rodríguez, according to Rita Wilson, *Angelitos negros* "is clearly based on the 1933 novel, *Imitation of Life*" by the United States writer, Fannie Hurst (1889-1968) (3). Hurst's novel was adapted into two Hollywood films by the same name. The first *Imitation of Life* film directed by John Stahal with Claudette Colbert was shot in 1934. The second *Imitation of Life* film directed by Douglas Sirk, featuring Lana Turner, was filmed in 1959 (Fischer 4). It should also be mentioned that there was a second *Angelitos negros* film shot in Mexico by Joselito Rodríguez in 1969 featuring Manuel López Ochoa and Martha Rangel with the African American actress Juanita Moore (Wilt). Juanita Moore played the victimized mammy in the 1959 *Imitation of Life*. It could be argued that the stories in *Angelitos negros* and

Imitation of life are two different stories at the pre-text level, but the subtexts are comparable in the way in which black people are coded. The stories are plotted differently, the roles are not quite the same, and the sets are dissimilar, nevertheless resemblance is found in comparing the message conveyed as far as what the filmmakers want one to believe and continue believing about blackness.

In *Angelitos negros*, non-black people, literally painted black, play two of the central "black" characters. The manner in which visibly black Mexicans are narrated exposes the ideology upon which the story is centered and it allows the placement of the film within the official discourse about visibly black people during the cultural phase of the Mexican Revolution where a whitening tendency dominates the narrative on nation. According to Jackson, while *mestizaje* is an indisputable process that black people have undergone, "the process of racial bleaching denies the Latin American black the recognizable African characteristics of his physical features and thus his black identity" (*The Black* 2). It is important to note also that this film is produced in a country that, according to its own official discourse, has imagined itself as non-white.

Angelitos negros belongs to a period in Mexican cinematography identified by Maximiliano Maza as *"Después de la Guerra"* (after the war). This period is dominated by films known as *Rumberas y Arrabal* (Maza). *Rumberas* refers to the *rumba*, an African Cuban rhythm adopted in Mexico that was born in the Cuban city slums that grew considerably at the end of the nineteenth century when some 250,000 slaves were freed and poured into the cities in search of employment (Alén 82). The *arrabal* refers mainly to Mexico City slums that grew quickly between 1940 and 1950. As they prepared for World War II, the industrialized nations had switched their production priorities from consumer goods to war goods.

One of the immediate results of this change in productivity was the industrialization of Mexico. The possibility of work attracted people from the rural areas to the city and they usually settled in the slums. *Rumberas* and *arrabal* films deal with life in the poor areas of the city and with the disorganized growing urbanization. These pictures are different from the *charro*[7] films that, according to Ricardo Pérez Monfort, dominated the industry from 1920 to 1946 (93). *Charro* films were used to cast an ideal image of the Mexican, an image that appears whiter than anything else and thereby negates the Africaness of Mexico and the African-chinaco element of the *charro* image and music.

Maza reports that between 1940 and 1950, the Mexican urban population grew more than ever. In 1946, Miguel Alemán Valdés became the first civilian president since 1932. Mexico's national infrastructure was greatly developed under his presidency. Also, according to Maza, President Alemán decreed *La Ley de la Industria Cinematográfica* (Law of the Film Industry) in an attempt to dissolve a monopoly on film-showing headed by the North American, William Jenkins. This strategy placed the film industry under government control and, perhaps unknowingly, established its bureaucratic foundations. Another setback for the dwindling Mexican film industry was the emergence of television in the early 1950s.[8]

With the end of the war, and as Hollywood re-entered the market full force, the position held by Mexican cinematography started to erode. Film companies in Mexico began to spend less per film in an effort to maintain the same levels of productivity reached during the war. The result of this approach was the proliferation of films known as *churros*, "low budget films made in a short time and of poor quality in general" (Maza). Pedro Infante, one of the central characters in *Angelitos Negros* and the indisputable star of the *cine de arrabal*, was the protagonist in *Los tres García* (1946) (*The Three Garcias*), *Nosotros los pobres* (1947) (*We the Poor*), *Ustedes los ricos* (1947) (*You the Rich*), *Dicen que soy mujeriego* (1948) (*They Say that I am a Womanizer*), and *Los tres Huastecos* (1948) (*The Three Huastecos*).

Two additional points should be made. *Angelitos negros* was one of three movies filmed in 1948 in which Infante was one of the principal characters. He was an idol, among the most popular male stars of the decade, and was considered a model of success (the provincial boy who comes to the country's capital and makes it big). In 1948, he was at the pinnacle of his acting and singing career. Loved by the masses, he was known as *el ídolo de las chorreadas* (something to the effect of "common-women's hero"). This last point is particularly important if one considers that his image in any movie of the time would attract a mass audience susceptible to persuasion by whatever role he represented.

According to David Wilt, in *Historia documental del cine mexicano*, Emilio García Riera says that, although *Angelitos negros* played only for two weeks in Mexico City, it was a big hit, so it can be said that the film had an immediate impact on a large number of people in the city. Wilt also mentioned that to find out how popular *Angelitos negros* really was, one would have to consider the number of subsequent runs in "neighborhood and provincial theatres," and obviously on television as well.

Angelitos negros, a cinematographic *churro*, is important because it may be the most widely-known of a group of films from the late 1940s and early 1950s that presented, as their central theme, the black question, such as *Negra consentida* (1948) (*Spoiled Black Woman*), *La negra Angustias* (1949) (*Angustias the Black Woman*), *Negro es mi color* (1951) (*Black is my Color*), and *Píntame angelitos blancos* (1954) (*Paint White Angels for Me*), among others. The "rediscovery" of visibly black Mexicans or mestizos in the mid forties, dealt a heavy blow to the myth of a purely Amerindian and "Spanish" *mestizaje*. It brought to the forefront the question of diversity in Mexico. Mexico was forced to revise its own discourse in order to get in step with its World War II allies.

That some sort of "new" awareness on the black question was arising in Mexico when Miguel Alemán Valdés was inaugurated president can be readily seen. The same year, 1946, the Mexican anthropologist and ethnologist, Gonzalo Aguirre Beltrán, returning from Northwestern University (USA), published *La población negra de México* (*The Black Population of Mexico*). In Aguirre Beltrán's words, "In spite of a good reception [*La población*] did not stimulate this interesting line of investigation" (11). Aguirre Beltrán continued his work and in 1948, he carried out an ethnographic investigation of the visibly black Mexican population in Cuijla, Guerrero (Aguirre 11). Curiously, that same year *Angelitos negros* was filmed and released, marking the genesis of a short-lived period of discursive acceptance of the existence of visibly black Mexicans, who, of course, knew their place.

Angelitos negros can be considered a piece of the propaganda used to deal with the black question in Mexico after the Second World War. According to Snead, a "film becomes 'propaganda' and no longer merely 'fiction' when its aim is to introduce or reinforce a set of political power relationships between social groups..." (140). *Angelitos negros* reinforces the power relationships instituted since colonial times between visibly black people and lighter skinned people by positioning the darker people as subservient.

Angelitos negros is of central import to the black experience and black identity in Mexico, and to the Mexican experience and identity as a whole since the majority of the population in Mexico are so called "mestizos" and the majority of Mexican mestizos, according to official and unofficial history, possess African blood in various degrees.

Angelitos negros allows the viewer to perceive the white aesthetic that dominates the official narrative of the period, and to see how visibly black Mexicans are still coded in and through this valuable piece of evidence of the eugenicist thinking instituted as an ideological perspective by José Vasconcelos.

Juan Carlos Ramérez Pimienta in his essay, "Del rancho al arrabal: guías para ayudar a formar un estado nación en el cine mexicano de La Época de Oro," (From the Ranch to the Ghetto: Guides to Help Form a Nation-State in the Mexican Cinema of the Golden Age) asks: "How...is it possible to think that the PRI-government did not design and implement a cultural policy to help it stay in power?" (Ramérez 211).[9] To speak of the possibility of a black experience and of a black identity in a country conceived as a mestizo-nation-in-the-process-of-whitening, may have been considered tantamount to an act of dissidence. This is probably why Joselito Rodríguez chose to deal with the subject in accordance with the official discourse. In *Angelitos Negros*, *criollos*, white-looking-mestizos and even Arabs are "white;" there are no Amerindians, except in their role as assimilated Indomestizos; and blacks are exotic, purely musical and passionate beings from a tropical paradigm (victimized servants, innocent children, or resigned friends) who are capable of unquestioning love and friendship for the "white" characters.

Angelitos negros asserts that class is the principal divider of Mexican people, and thus minimizes the "racial" friction that nevertheless exists in the house where the drama develops. Rodríguez's story proposes that in Mexican society at large, there are good, at least acceptable, relations between the "social" groups; and that the relations in the central part of the story, the domestic situation, can and will be resolved by a higher type of understanding obtained by Ana Luisa, the perpetrator of the conflict.

Angelitos negros was supposed to be an "anti-racist" film. However, "real" black people play minor characters, as is the case of Chimy Monterrey who plays Fernando. He is a character capable of supporting open discrimination, as his due, without complaint. Fernando is the ever-understanding friend of José Carlos. Snead has identified a similar role as "the loyal sidekick/retainer" (142). Emilia Guiú plays the central character, Ana Luisa. Rita Montaner, a "white" Cuban actress heavily painted to appear black plays "Mercé." Pedro Infante plays José Carlos Ruiz; and Titina Romay, heavily painted as well, plays Belén (she is Joselito Rodriguez, the film director's daughter).

José Carlos suffers "the prejudice of having no prejudice." He is oblivious of non-white people's plight against the white superiority syndrome. He is capable of "listening" to all sides but does not perceive as racist the attitudes before him. The film suggests that he is a good-natured person, unmindful of racial discrimination. He is literally blinded by his "deep love" for the blond looking Ana Luisa, while he is unaware of the unwavering and understanding love the visibly black Mexican woman, Isabel, has had for him secretly over the years. He acknowledges that visibly black Mexicans are as they are because that is "the way God made them." He has a sort of puppy love for Mercé. Although she is his elder, he calls her "my little tar ball," "my little chocolate bar," "my little pile of soot," "my little chunk of tar," "little cinnamon flower," "ugly negra," "fine little black one made from the little charcoal that makes diamonds," among other names. At the level of subtext, no matter how "sweet" these names may appear, they position Mercé in opposition to Ana Luisa.

Conversely, he calls Ana Luisa "Goldilocks," "Blondie," "the most beautiful girl in the city," and compares her with the sun itself (just as Mercé does; this points out the existence of a collective belief). Moreover, his supposed best friend, who according to him is almost his "brother," carries water (while José Carlos' hands are free) to wash José Carlos and scrub his back. He is a kind of mediator who accepts things as if prescribed by a divine force. Even José Carlos' love for Ana Luisa is presented as divine. He is capable of suffering the unthinkable, and of accepting the suffering of visibly black people given his love for Ana Luisa, a type of love that in the end of the *churro* succeeds.

The Mexican government went so far as to create a censorship organism to ban movies considered defamatory (García Riera 148). It is paradoxical to find that while official Mexico noted the way Mexicans were portrayed by Hollywood, it was incapable of recognizing the manner in which visibly black Mexicans were presented to the viewer in *Angelitos negros* by Mexicans whose overwhelming majority, as mentioned above, are non-whites, according to the cosmic race myth.

Snead identifies three strategies to forge and reinforce stereotypes on race: mythification, marking, and omission. He proposes that film is never one person's story but "is always typical, broadcasting certain codes about social status and interrelationships" (143).

In *Angelitos negros*, the viewer is exposed to "mythification" when José Carlos is elevated in the introductory scenes of the film. He is clean and elegantly dressed in a cashmere suit, white starched shirt, and tie (as a gentleman was supposed to dress in the Mexico of the late 1940s). He has a shiny late-model convertible and is confidently buying a newspaper in front of a Mediterranean-style house, indicating a well-to-do neighborhood.

The scenes are well illuminated like a sunny day. José Carlos is overly cheerful, thus denoting a person who has no apparent worries beyond enjoying life. He portrays a secure individual who feels good enough to approach another upper-class individual without formal introduction, namely the visibly blond Ana Luisa who has come out of the Mediterranean-style mansion to hail a taxi.

Fernando, on the other hand, would not dream of approaching a white rich woman, knowing that he would have no chance for a positive result, and that to do so would be an open invitation for real trouble. Yet, Isabel, a mulatto singer, who has worked for years along with Fernando and the famous singer José Carlos, has been secretly in love with José Carlos. Her broken heart is understood to be a normal occurrence, even by Fernando (a visibly black man who is portrayed as her confidant or brother), as some sort of predestined penance. The visibly black characters are presented as other than individuals, as if tied by blood and destiny and desirous of assimilation into the dominant group. Their aesthetic is the white aesthetic. All visibly black people in the film seem to be destined to suffer due to their color. As Snead states, "[t]he coding of blacks in film, as in the wider society, involves a history of images and signs associating black skin color with servile behavior and marginal status" (142).

According to Snead, mythification, the magnification of the film image, "can both elevate and degrade," and he explains that in fact both "properties are interdependent" since the same "language that magnifies white heroes reduces black people" (143). In *Angelitos negros*, "white" characters in positions of control are juxtaposed with the likes of a mulatto old woman who has always been and continues to be, until her death, a live-in housemaid. As the narrative unfolds, the viewer learns that Mercé's life is a tragedy, a story of dependence. The film introduces Mercé in a large mansion, rendering her character even more insignificant, and she is contrasted with her boss Ana Luisa (Guiú), a young blonde, well-educated woman presented as the owner of the house. Snead elucidates: "soon, by mythification and repetition, filmed images become models, positive or negative, for behavior, describing structures, limits, and an overall repertoire from which viewers in the real world select their actions and opinions" (143).

The second of Snead's tactics for coding is "marking." According to Snead, "Marking the black allows the viewer to 'register' the image" (145). He explains that this is necessary due to the fact that a strict definition of what "blackness" is, cannot be provided. He says that: "The terms of racial identity—'white' and 'black'—denote not any one thing, but a whole range of possibilities, all defined, not positively by being this or that, but negatively, by not being 'white' " (145). In *Angelitos negros*, Mercé, the nanny, Belén, the tragic mulatto daughter, and Isabel, the mulatto afflicted by her one-sided love for José Carlos, are played by non-black people marked by heavy black paint. According to Snead, marking meets the "needs of the image-making rhetoric" and by making black representation as black as possible eliminates any ambiguity (145). Marking through contrasting black and white colors in clothing or by the use of light has been used "for stereotypical and ideological purposes" as well (145). The secondary black characters are dressed in various scenes with white clothes to highlight their darkness and they are further marked as they speak *jarocho*, or African Mexican dialect and sing, dance, and play African Mexican music in a supposedly white environment.

The third manner in which stereotypes are cast in this film is "omission." *Angelitos negros* omits any reference to visibly black Mexicans who are not children, servants or entertainers. Snead found that in Hollywood "[f]rom the earliest days of film, omission was the method of choice in designing and tailoring mass images of black people" (147). This perspective may be applied to *Angelitos negros.*

Notable is that the story takes place in Mexico City in the late 1940s and that psychologically and socially urban "visibly" black Mexicans of that period are not portrayed as significantly better off than urban blacks during the colonial period. The fact that historically prominent visibly black Mexicans have existed, such as Yanga, José María Morelos y Pavón, Vicente Guerrero, Vicente Riva Palacio, Lázaro Cárdenas and the *chinacos,* to mention a few, does not appear anywhere in the film. The viewer cannot even imagine it despite the fact that, by the time *Angelitos negros* was filmed, at least two states of the nation were named after African Mexicans and that African Mexicans were the leaders of the freedom movement, presidents, and cannon fodder, not to mention mothers, wives, sisters and daughters whose blood has shaped a substantial part of the mestizo nation.

Angelitos negros artificially separates the Mexican world of the late 1940s into two well defined paradigms: that of a few markedly identified mulattoes who live tragic lives, and that of people who appear to be non-black and who, for the most part, are well-to-do. The reason this inaccurate representation of black people has received no noticeable objection from the viewers at large may be derived from the fact that most Mexicans mistakenly believe they have little to do, if at all, with Africa.

In *Angelitos negros*, white-looking people are mythified while markedly black mulattoes are denigrated. In this manner, the superiority of non-blacks is confirmed. Now, logical contradictions and historical inaccuracies aside, how could such misrepresentations of visibly black Mexicans be of any importance in a realm where the official discourse affirms, through all means of persuasion available, that black people are nearly extinct or "integrated?"

The academically documented "discovery" in the mid 1940s of enclaves in Mexico where black people, allegedly due to isolation, had preserved their African characteristics, and the production of *Angelitos negros* among other films of the epoch on the black theme, leads one to assume that the system enlisted and supported cinematography to continue to disseminate the notion that the whitening process in Mexico was still ongoing. The possibility of engaging a problem long forgotten officially, or set aside by the myth of *mestizaje*, was neutralized through cinematic rhetoric. The collective lie of a binary *mestizaje* exclusive of its African root was reinforced in Mexico this time through one of the most powerful means of mass persuasion.

The type of narrative found in *Angelitos negros* reproduces and reinforces cinematic stereotypes and is aimed at penetrating susceptible viewers who want-to-be-white (or those who believe they are non-blacks). This type of cultural text allows them to perceive themselves as they wish to be seen by visibly black people, namely as superior. "Indeed, racism in the cinema might be described as the tendency to recycle certain ethnic codes, already familiar to a series of privileged viewers, in order to reinforce their familiarity, despite the changes that may have gone on in the real world" (Snead 142).

Mercé, the concubine/servant/mammy/house-maid, while repeating and reinforcing the stereotype of "Aunt Jemima," also shields it from historical change. Every time the film is shown, unless the audience has been trained to question its propagandistic essence, it reiterates stereotypes of visibly black people. It promotes while it perpetuates a sort of dialogue between viewer and image based on power relationships (where visibly black people are forever trapped at the bottom of the physical, psychological and social scale) based on black phobia and a white aesthetic.

In Mexico at large, as a colonial legacy, one of the most derogatory names to be called is "indio" (Indian). This means to be ugly, and barbaric; it means to be an outsider, the "other." But an even worse insult, another colonial legacy, is to be called *negro* (black).

Afro-phobia seems to be common among Mexican mestizos, notwithstanding the likelihood that they are direct descendants of the *mezclas* who were African Mexicans. This may be understood if one takes into consideration that while a considerable percentage of Mexicans are in fact just as "black" as anything else, visibly black women and men in Mexico, as well as in other parts of the continent, have been made to feel inferior and have thereby been physically and sexually abused. In Mexico, the most common way to escape slavery, literally, was through miscegenation. Thus, anyone capable of "passing" and liberating oneself from the "stigma" of blackness, as a matter of life and freedom, learned to follow the whitening trend.

In *Angelitos negros*, the complexity of this Mexican Afro-phobia can be observed in the blond Ana Luisa, a Mexican twist of the stereotype of the tragic mulatto identified by Shohat (195). One learns early in the story that Ana Luisa is in fact a mulatto and that she "really" does not know that she is part black. She is capable of accepting the services provided by Mercé, but she treats her as an infant even though Mercé has raised her. Ana Luisa also discriminates against José Carlos' friends. In a scene where Fernando is introduced to her, she refuses to shake his extended hand, turns her back on him and leaves the room as if not wanting to breath the same air and share the same space.

Ana Luisa despises everything black, even berating José Carlos on one occasion for painting himself black in order to perform on stage. She accepts him as a performer but she does not hide her dislike of the African (Latin) American music and African (Latin) American choreography of the show, and expresses her desire to see him as what he "is." She clearly has a superior attitude while watching the performance. Her Afro-phobia escalates when, after a long and successful acting tour of Latin America (with seven months of a seemingly wonderful stay in Buenos Aires), they come back happily to Mexico City. Thereafter, she has a mulatto daughter. She does not want any part of her daughter and she accuses José Carlos of "dirtying" her life with black blood. The viewer is presented with the perspective that if one is a well-to-do white person, it is an understandable tragedy to have a "black" child.

Ana Luisa suffers tremendously and shuts herself in to suffer her "misfortune" alone. Curiously, although she commits different degrees of child-abuse, all characters show a great deal of understanding towards her, including the well-respected catholic priest. As mentioned before, the priest counsels José Carlos and Mercé that Ana Luisa should not be told that she is a mulatto due to her fragile emotional condition for she may go crazy or loose her life.[10] Mercé begs José Carlos not to say anything, to spare her "beautiful" daughter any more pain. José Carlos agrees to keep the secret and endures Ana Luisa's abuse due to his "love" and devotion.

The story climaxes when Mercé rolls down the stairs as a consequence of having been slapped on the face by Ana Luisa. José Carlos and the priest are on the second floor and José Carlos screams, "No! She is your mother!" Ana Luisa is startled and looks toward the priest. The priest comes down to hold her and confirms non-verbally what José Carlos has just said. Mercé dies as a consequence of the fall, at which point Ana Luisa "comes" to her senses. She promises to change and take care of her daughter. José Carlos, of course, exonerates Ana Luisa, his "Goldilocks." Ana Luisa literally gets away with murder in *Angelitos negros*.[11]

Until the last few scenes of this film, Ana Luisa, the "tragic mulatto," does not know about her blackness and everybody is sympathetic towards her. This understanding continues even when Ana Luisa explodes, verbally and physically abusing Mercé who has cared for her since birth. Ana Luisa does not have to deal with "passing" as white, for in the end, and according to the official ideology in Mexico disseminated during the cultural phase of the Revolution, to look non-black is to look "beautiful." Ana Luisa has been saved and her implied sentence is to have to accept her "black" daughter who nevertheless is on her way to whiteness.

The black stereotypes and white mythification marked by cinematic technique in this Mexican *churro* connect with other images and narratives distributed in Mexico since colonial times that were adopted officially as discourse on nation at the onset of the cultural phase of the Revolution. Once the connection is made, and codes formed, the real world is bypassed. The cinematic narrative is pleasurable to the target audience (all of those susceptible viewers wanting to be, at least in the mind, non-black) displacing the necessity of verifying the codes. As Snead has said, "[s]o the history of black film stereotypes is the history of the denial of history in favor of an artificially constructed general truth about the unchanging black character" (139).

The Mexico of the late forties dealt in this manner with the "rediscovery" of blacks. In a way, it told the public that everything was okay, that "black" blacks were few and that soon they would be willingly and happily assimilated. This discourse was "convincing" enough for its allies as well. It helped Mexico reinforce and preserve its "progressive" profile in the modern world, an appearance acquired as a result of its stance during WWII.

Today, one of the problems with *Angelitos negros* is that it continues to be copied and shown without warning. Caution ought to be given, as to the negative effects—psychological, societal and political—the message in the film has had. This is of particular importance for a population affected by the "false memory syndrome."[12]

Notes

[1] Maximiliano Maza, in an effort to dispel confusion as to whether all black-and-white motion pictures are in fact from the Golden Age of Mexican cinematography, creates a sub-category he calls the "Golden Years of the Golden Age." He explains, "Our television culture has conditioned us to consider any Mexican black-and-white film as part of The Golden Age. The true 'golden years' of the Golden Age would coincide with the Second World War (1939-1945)," (Maza 1). Maza says "Mexican cinematographic production had reached a high level by 1939. In fact 'The Golden Age' began years before WWII, a factor often cited as a direct cause" (*Introducción*). Thus, according to Maza, the Golden Age began well before the war, but the best years, what he calls "The Golden Years" nevertheless coincide with the war.

[2] Cinematographic message here is the capacity of film to transmit an idea with the advantages that are particular to this medium. Film has the capacity to influence a frame through sound, predisposing the audience to receive the message in an intended manner. It has the capacity to create an ambience to manipulate the general mood by the intensity, scarcity, or absence of light. It has the advantage of plotting the story in the style most convenient for a given cultural context in order to enable a "dialogue" with the audience across space and time (as an example, a film from another epoch, from another country, from another language, is capable of making us feel angry, melancholic, sad, happy or totally sexual). Excellent examples of this way of projecting a message to the masses are *Cantinflas'* movies that "talked the talk and walked the walk" of the Mexican *pelado*. These films reached people from Chicago,

Los Angeles, Florida, and all over Latin America where there was access to TV or to itinerant theaters.

[3] Academic investigation on the Africaness of Mexican *mestizaje* is in its early stages. Most of the work being done is relatively recent and is in the areas of history, linguistics, anthropology, ethnology, music and dance. A considerable portion of that investigation relies heavily on "non-Mexican" perspectives and "non-Mexicans" are doing an important part of the work. This may be understood if one considers that black Mexicans are part of the greater phenomenon known as the "Maafa" or black holocaust. There is no local or international criticism to be found about the manner in which people of African descent have been and are portrayed and characterized in Mexican cinematography.

[4] James Snead defines film as a "series of recorded and repeatable moving images that aims to make a viewer believe in the story or reality it claims to portray" (134). This definition is hereby adopted.

[5] *La negra Angustias* (1949) is another film of this type. It is based on Francisco Rojas González's 1944 novel by the same name. Angustias is the daughter of a mulatto road bandit who has been imprisoned until the time she meets him when he is old. She grows up in the Morelos' mountains under the care of an Indian medicine woman. As the Revolution sweeps the area, and as a consequence of hurting someone while trying to defend herself from being raped, she joins the war and becomes a feared *coronela* (colonel) due to her innate daringness and bravado. However, toward the end, the audience learns that one of her greatest desires has been to learn to read and write Spanish. Also, she falls in love with her weakling *criollo* teacher and ends up living in a room in Mexico City with her whitened infant son. The teacher collects her pension and recognizes her only as a lover; actually he is ashamed of their relationship.

[6] In "Las mitologías del cine mexicano," Carlos Monsiváis points out, "The same as everywhere, in México, US film industry is the inevitable model…everything is learned from Hollywood…" (2).

[7] The *charro* image is the "sanitized" version of the *chinaco* image.

[8] In the case of *Angelitos negros*, the emergence of television would be favorable. The movie was shown on TV often and thus it reached a wider audience than it would have reached otherwise. It should be mentioned also that in the 1980s the story was made into a soap opera of some 120 half-hour episodes featuring Manuel López Ochoa, and that it was transmitted outside Mexico.

[9] In 1946, during the government of Miguel Alemán Valdés, the *Partido Revolucionario Mexicano* (PRM) (Mexican Revolutionary Party) became the PRI.

[10] Ana Luisa's condition in the film can be understood as a metaphor of the modern nation that sees itself as too fragile to confront its own origins just yet:

under the white aesthetic, in order to be made to appear strong before the world, it must ignore its African heritage. To do otherwise would be to create a national catastrophe where the nation could lose its own Eurocentric identity.

[11] This can be seen as a metaphor of the "murdering" or erasure of the Africaness of Mexicaness.

[12] This concept was adopted from a commentary published in *The Vancouver Sun*, Thursday, December 23, 1999, E 1. People affected with this condition have been persuaded that something that exists never was. Gorostiza's *El color de nuestra piel*, is a prime representation of this condition that affects Mexican mestizos whose views are shaped by black phobia and a white aesthetic.

Five

Modern National Discourse and *La muerte de Artemio Cruz*: The Illusory "Death" of African Mexican Lineage[1]

> The ideal of *mestizaje*, so pejoratively translated as miscegenation, was based in the reality of mixed races to which the positivists ascribed different virtues and failings, and which had to amalgamate if anything like national unity was to be produced. Unity, in positivist rhetoric, was not so much a political or economic concept as it was biological. Since growth meant modernization and Europeanization, the most extreme ideologues (like Argentina's Domingo F. Sarmiento) advocated a combined policy of white immigration and Indian or Black removal, while others...[as the Mexican ideologues] settled for redeeming the "primitive" races through miscegenation and ideological whitening.
>
> Doris Sommer

The modern Mexican nation emerged in the third decade of the twentieth century during the cultural phase of the Mexican Revolution. The *criollo* (white) controlled government disseminated officially the myth that *mestizos* were the offspring of Spaniards and Amerindians exclusively, in that order. Thereafter, this discourse was reproduced and reinforced through various means of mass persuasion, including the novel, until 1968.

The black African heritage of Mexican *mestizaje* was replaced in the collective memory and national imaginary with José Vasconcelos' "cosmic race" myth. This philosophy, a continuation of Spanish colonial beliefs, codified blacks as tame and their genes as recessive. By insisting that Spanish genes were dominant and that black African genes were recessive in the mestizo, *criollos,* as supposed heirs of the Spanish genes, "legitimated" a paternity claim; hence, a protagonist role in carving out the Mexican nation. This enabled them to transfer historical glory to their name. The history of *cimarronaje* was erased and African Mexican national heroes were whitened, thus African Mexican national achievements became *criollo* based.

According to Vasconcelos' creed, exposed in the first forty pages of his *La raza cósmica,* the black characteristics of the Mexican were receding through natural selection. In his Christian-rooted vision, "beauty" was overpowering "ugliness" and the mestizo population was steadily and eagerly whitening. The modern nation builders adopted Vasconcelos' views as the unequivocal road toward modernization. *La muerte de Artemio Cruz* (1962) (*The Death of Artemio Cruz*), by Carlos Fuentes, reintroduces and reinforces the myth of the Mexican populace's willing submission to whitening.

In this canonized post-modern novel, the central character, a post-revolution Mexican prototype, on a level, appears as a "mestizo" oblivious of his African family tree; but as he reels through memory from his deathbed, the reader is informed that in the depth of his heart he despises his negritude. He is convinced that "the whiter the better." *La muerte* is read in this study as a link in the chain of canonized *criollo* works reflecting the cosmic race-discourse on nation whose iron-like determination, from the start, was the cleansing of blackness from the population, if at least psychologically.

La muerte continues the construction of a false national identity. The novel depicts and perpetuates stereotypes of blacks. It posits that for black characters to be rebellious, or to show intelligence, they have to be whitened. *La muerte* ignores that black Africans from the beginning of the *Maafa* or Black Holocaust have revolted. Alive in the late sixteenth and early seventeenth century, Yanga, the maroon leader in Veracruz, the home state of the protagonist anti-hero of the novel, is a case in point.

La muerte is read in light of pertinent portions of Octavio Paz' "*Los hijos de la Malinche*" (1950), *El perfil del hombre y la cultura en México* (1934) by Samuel Ramos, and *La raza cósmica* (1925) by José Vasconcelos to track down the codification of blackness under its various Mexican signifiers.   The aim is to exhibit the intertextuality of these canonized *criollo* works, pillars of the modern nation, and disclose how they codify the African Mexican Experience.

La muerte uses *chingar* as substance in constructing Cruz' character (143-47).   It thereby makes him a prototype of the Mexican *pelado* as pointed out by both Remigio Paez, the catholic priest, who brokers his marriage to the *criolla* Catalina (47), and Cruz himself (276). Regarding the Mexican *pelado*, Ana María Prieto Hernández reveals, "*zaragates, guachinangos, zaramullos, zánganos, ínfima plebe, chusma, peladaje* [plural pejorative of *pelado*] or "*léperos*" were the postcolonial names given to the various mestizos of African descent (17-19) (emphasis mine).   These euphemisms replaced part of the "sixty-four" Spanish colonial categories used to refer to a person's degree of African heritage (Davis 37).

"Los hijos de la Malinche," a parody of *los hijos de la chingada* (sons of the raped African Mexican woman), exposes that *chingar* is a "vulgar" word (Paz 67), and that the general population is master of its usage (Paz 67).   It posits that *chingar* may be of Aztec origin (Paz 68). Thereby, it cleanses *léperos* or *pelados* from their African heritage. "Los hijos" claims the *mestizo, lépero or pelado* as the offspring of Spaniards and Amerindians, in that order.

The Malinche,[2] a synonym of national treason, embodied in a pre-Hispanic born Amerindian woman who gives into Hernán Cortés, is inserted in the place of *la chingada*.   Through its thesis, besides glorifying the *criollo* and marking the Amerindian genes of the mestizo as inherently "malinchista," it blocks the possibility of establishing the relations between *La chingada*, her Africaness and the African Kimbundu cradle of the verb *chingar* (Pérez Fernández).

"Los hijos de la Malinche" replaces the maroon history of mestizaje in the national imaginary. It omits mestizaje's African heritage.   "Los hijos" annuls the connection between Africans, African Mexicans, *alvaradeños, jarochos, chinacos, léperos,* or *pelados.*   "Los hijos" is another vehicle of cultural misappropriation. It confuses ownership of the verb *chingar* and blurs the African origins and identity of the Mexican *mezclas* or *mestizos.*

"Los hijos" fuses all "social" classes through the word *chingar.*   It presents Mexico and Mexicaness as one; this underlines the fallacy of Mexico as a racial paradise.   By omitting its Africaness, it creates a "rightful" and preferential space for the *criollo* within a culture constructed by the Other. Ted Vincent exhibits the two separate worlds constructed in Mexico during the colonial period: the Spanish-*criollo* world marked by the minuet, wine and white bread; and the *mezcla* world marked by La bamba, tequila, and corn tortillas (5). For "Los hijos," Mexicaness, embodied in the *mestizo*, has Spanish and Amerindian roots alone, in that order.

"Los hijos" follows the "psychoanalytical profile" of the *pelado* in *El perfil*. After calling the *pelado* "fauna," *El perfil* characterizes the *pelado* as "a being without principles, generally mistrusting, full of bluster and cowardly" (Ramos 76). *El perfil* manifests that as a subject, the *pelado* "lacks all human values" and that in fact he is "incapable of acquiring" said values (Ramos 76). *El perfil's* evaluation of the *pelado* is linked to Vasconcelos and his philosophy on education (Muñoz 24). *El perfil* forwards the perspective that Mexican culture is a culture of cultures whose most valuable manifestation is the *criollo* culture. In *La muerte*, the protagonist recognizes Mexico as "a thousand countries under one name" (274) where *criollos* are the mark of civilization (50).

Cruz is narrated as a dying seventy-one year old (16) Mexican of African lineage who does not identify with his African heritage (276). He is the bastard son of a certain "Isabel Cruz, Cruz Isabel," a Mulatto woman whose true name is unknown (314). Cruz' father, Anastasio Menchaca, is a *criollo* who during the *Porfiriato* had been a powerful landowner. Cruz is six feet tall and weighs about 174 pounds (247). He has "pronounced features" (41), a wide nose (9) graying curly hair (16, 251) that once was black (314). He has dark skin (16), as the "very dark" skin color of his son (168). He has green eyes that project a cold, unwavering look (171), an energetic mouth, wide forehead, protruding cheekbones (149) and thick lips (115).

Cruz becomes Lieutenant Colonel during the armed phase of the Revolution. Through his cunning marriage to a *criolla*, the sister of a fellow soldier executed by a firing squad at the end of the armed conflict, he turns out to be first, a landowner and administrator, and later, a newspaper magnate and a millionaire by brokering government concessions to foreigners.

In *La muerte*, the images are patchy and colored in a cubist fashion. For instance, when Cruz tells himself:

> Although I don't want it to, something shines insistently next to my face; something that reproduces itself behind my closed eyelids: a fugue of black lights and blue circles. I contract the face muscles, I open the right eye and I see it reflected in the glass incrustations of a woman's purse (...)

I am this old man with the features shattered by the irregular glass squares.
(9)

The physical and ideological descriptions of the characters are introduced in scattered fragments and clues throughout the novel, as a puzzle that must be assembled. In the case of Cruz, this renders his heritage confusing. The analytical Afrocentric reader must amass the fragments to realize Cruz is an African Mexican. The level of difficulty of this decoding task is evidenced by the scattered page numbers where Cruz' characteristics and features are introduced bit by bit nonchalantly: 276, 324, 247, 41, 9, 16, 251, 314, 168, 171, 149, 115, and 316, among others.

The reader is forced to travel back and forth in time. The images evoked by Cruz flash in and out of focus. Time, space, physical and metaphysical barriers are shattered as the plot develops in Cruz' psyche. He brings the past to the present at will. One case in point is when he recalls his childhood, as in a close-up scene, and transports the reader to a different place in time (271).

The past and present dissolve into one plane when pain brings Cruz out of his lethargy and he becomes aware of the presence of others in the room (116). An uncertain future intermingles with the present when Cruz foresees what may happen (247). *La muerte* penetrates the memory of the reader lost in trying to put together the pieces and unexpectedly, subliminally lays an Eurocentrically idealized world in the place of historical facts. Thus, what never happened replaces maroon history. The novel shapes a national imaginary according to *criollo* beliefs.

Julio Ortega interprets *La muerte* as "the first product of Latin American post-modernity" and as "a disenchanted reading of compulsive modernity" (2). This is correct to a point. *La muerte* provides a "fresh" look at the Revolution and indicts the corrupted patriarchal system. Thereby, it passes within the guise of the long awaited voice of self—criticism of a decadent structure.

On a level, *La muerte* casts the illusion of condemning the existing political structure: the entrenched PRI[3] system that from the onset of the cultural phase of the Revolution sought total control and power over the people. *La muerte* condemns the Mexican post-revolution's social situation in part; nonetheless, at a subliminal level, it endorses the color divide imposed since the colonial period.

Through a close review, the Afrocentric reader is forced to question the authenticity of the character ascribed to Cruz as an African Mexican in modern Mexico, particularly in light of the prevalent *criollo* mentality that loathed even a drop of "visible" blackness in a person.

Had racism subsided in Mexico by 1920 as to allow a visibly black person to rise "freely" from rags to riches? How many visibly black Mexicans can be found as tycoons in the Mexico of the first half of the twentieth century? If "it always has been an object of the novel to tell the other version of history, particularly starting after the nineteeth century" as Carlos Fuentes has declared (Güemes 2), would it not have been more true to life to have made the antihero a *criollo*?

Why make a "pelado" (47, 276) or mestizo of African descent the villain? Is the novel repeating and reinforcing the white myth of the "evil nature" of African blood? Is *La muerte* reintroducing and reinforcing the Eurocentric colonial stereotypes of *los hijos de la chingada* and the *pelados* found in *La raza cósmica*, *El perfil*, and "Los hijos"?

Snead clarifies that mass-produced images have political, ideological, and psychological effects upon an audience's beliefs and actions (132). Also, he states "Stereotypes ultimately connect to form larger complexes of symbols and connotations. These codes then begin to form a kind of 'private conversation' among themselves without needing to refer back to the real world for their facticity" (141).

La muerte gets close to the origins of *chingar* and the *pelado*. It nearly makes the connections between the *mestizo*, his language, his worldview and his African heritage. This may have enabled a fuller explanation of the Mexican character[4] and his sense of humor as early as 1962.

However, *La muerte* continues the same *criollo* aesthetic found in *La raza cósmica*, *El perfil,* and "Los hijos." Cruz is characterized as a mestizo who, notwithstanding, or because of his visible African heritage, the knowledge of his birth, and his having been raised in an African Mexican environment until the age of fourteen, has virtually repressed his black legacy.

It is a sign of indecency for Cruz "to live and die in [the] Negro shack" of his lineage and cultural heritage (276). *La muerte* whitens Cruz' by making him particularly proud of his *criollo* identity. Cruz expresses that he has conquered "decency" for his children. He expects them to thank him for making them "respectable people," and keeping them out of the "Negro shack" (276).

According to Snead, a work "becomes 'propaganda' and no longer merely 'fiction' when its aim is to introduce or reinforce a set of political power relationships between social groups" (140). In *La muerte*, Mexicans whose African lineage is openly identified are characterized as rootless (302), backward, submissive, tame and servile (302-03). They are caricatured as simple, as jungle beings (302) with an endless sexual appetite (279, 288-89), as possessing an innate musicality (288), and as having a natural predisposition to relax (287). This is remarkable when juxtaposed to *criollo* portrayal. *Criollos* are conceived as civilized (50), rooted to the land (48); as history makers (35), with an identity (50); as having feelings, ideals, and even as being chivalrous at the moment of defeat (50). This perception echoes *El perfil's* notions about *criollo* supremacy. The Spaniards in *La muerte* are capable of understanding, and of sacrificing body and soul for family and beliefs (50, 54, 103).

Snead explains, "'Codes' are not singular portrayals of one thing or another, but larger complex relationships" (142). He exposes how these relationships, under the will, imagination and ideological slant of the narrative maker, may "present fantasy or an ideal world that has nothing to do with the real world" as if it were the real world (134).

According to Lanin A. Gyurko, Cruz is developed as a "single character, powerful and complex enough to be convincing, not only as an individual but also as a national symbol" (30). In *La muerte*, this national character is imagined by his uncle as a black Moses (285). But paradoxically, and as if marked by his African blood, Cruz is constructed as an innate traitor, a despicable being: polygamous (122), immoral, greedy (15-16), treacherous (24-25), cowardly, and corrupted (16, 21, 50, 56).

Cruz is incapable of caring about high revolutionary ideals, or country (56). He is the opposite of José María Tecla Morelos y Pavón (Vargas) and Vicente "el negro" Guerrero, each a Black Moses. In Gyurko's words: "Cruz is literally an *hijo de la chingada*. Violation gave him life —rape of a slave woman by his father, Anastasio Menchaca; violation pervades his life, and violation (mental and physical) characterizes his death" (35). For Gyurko, on the symbolic level, Cruz is a metaphor for the Frozen Revolution and a nation that "slavishly imitates the value systems of European and North American nations" (39).

Cruz is rich, powerful and married into a *criollo* family. However, it is made obvious that these "attributes," *per se,* cannot remove the color line that marginalizes him throughout the story. He enters a marriage where the color divide is kept and cultured within the relationship (103).[5]   All the power Artemio Cruz has is not enough to free his conscience from the knowledge of being "the Other," even at home with his wife and daughter (31-32).

This very power, impressive physique and ruthless character, given him so lavishly, mark Artemio Cruz and make him stand out as a whitened black (33). Cruz never gains control of his life, although a millionaire. This creates the illusion that the *criollos* he wishes to emulate are naturally superior to him and those he is the prototype of, nonwhite Mexicans (32, 33, 50). Snead identifies mythification, marking and omission as three particular tactics to forge and perpetuate black stereotypes (143). He points out that to make whites appear more civilized, powerful and important, they are shown in contrast to subservient blacks. *La muerte* does this.

Lunero, Cruz' Uncle, is a well-tamed and *criollo*-loyal young Mulatto who quietly accepts his fate (284). He is still in bondage at the beginning of the twentieth century (295). He silently tolerates the sexual rape and physical abuse of his sister, Isabel, Cruz' mother, by the master, Cruz' father. Lunero helps Isabel during Cruz' birth (314). But he does nothing and stays quiet when the master, a known rapist of nonwhite women (229), beats Isabel with a stick and runs her off the property in his presence (286, 306). Lunero is unbelievably good and incapable of running away. He invents work to support his masters' household (285, 303) when they have become poor due to the war. He is very protective of Cruz and takes care of him for fourteen years even though, or perhaps due to Cruz' being a lighter black.

Jackson points out that discrimination, based on place of origin, color of skin, social class, and religious beliefs, has been instrumental in developing a narrative that depicts black people in "one dimension racist images," as purely sensuous, as merely musical savages waiting to be saved from their supposed incapacity to reason, and from their entirely emotional realm (*Black Image* 46)

Lunero is narrated as having the rhythm in him (287-88). Every afternoon he sings to young Cruz the songs brought by Lunero's father from Santiago de Cuba "when the war broke out and the families moved to Veracruz along with their servants" (286). He is a prisoner of fear and nostalgia. He fears the New World: the sierra, the Amerindians, and the plateau (302); and is nostalgic of the continent where "one like him would be able to get lost in the jungle and say that he had returned" (302).

Jackson exhibits that Latin American literature, guided by the white aesthetic, caricatures blacks, presents blacks as easily corruptible, with an endless sexual appetite, as possessing an innate musicality, as having a natural predisposition to relax, as inherently drunkard, as polygamous, as irresponsible parents and as devil-like (*Black Image* 49-59).

According to Snead:

> The history that whites have made (…) empties black skin of any historical or material reference, except as former slaves. The notion of the eternal black "character" is invented to justify the enforced economic disadvantage that we enjoy (or don't enjoy)(…). [B]lacks' behavior is portrayed as being unrelated to the history that whites have trapped them in. Let me repeat: that behavior is being portrayed as something static, enduring, and unchangeable, unrelated to the history that whites have trapped them in. Blacks are seen as ahistorical. (139)

Isabel Cruz or Cruz Isabel, Artemio Cruz' mother, is a woman without a fixed name that appears in the narrative only as a vessel to bring another *hijo de la chingada* into the world (314). Although she appears fleetingly, she leaves the impression of being nothing more than a victim, a fearful presence incapable of making a sound even at the moment of delivery. Jackson has found that even in cases where blacks are defended, they are depicted, among other ways, as backward, submissive, tame, and servile ("Black Phobia" 467).

In *La muerte,* African Mexicans seem to inhabit Veracruz, and not to extend beyond the sierra. The hacienda of Cocuya is full of blacks (295), "Negroid" people (289), and "… clear eyed Mulattoes with skin the color of pine nuts" who were offspring of the "Indian and Mulatto women that went around bearing them" (289). One learns about blacks "brought to the tropical plantations with their hair straightened by the daring Indian women that offered their hairless sexual parts as a victory redoubt over the curly haired race" (279).

In contrast to *La muerte's* narrative, it is well documented that black Africans of the Diaspora were taken all over New Spain wherever there was mining, farming, ranching, factories, domestic work, or transportation of goods. History shows that African Mexicans, the infamous *mezclas*, became the majority of today's *mestizos* (Aguirre Beltrán 276).

History confirms that the *mezclas* or mestizos of African descent fought valiantly under the name of *"chinacos"* and *"pintos"* during the War of Independence (1810-1821) (Riva Palacio's *Calvario*; Díaz, xviii). It archives that later, they fought against the French and defeated them in Puebla (5 May 1862). History records that the *chinaco* and *pinto* liberals followed the French into the interior of the country and, against all odds, defeated and expelled them from Mexican national territory three years later.

"The omission of the black [heroes], then, has meant the presence of the stereotype" (Snead 147). *La muerte's* reintroduction and reinforcement of black stereotypes does not end there. Cruz' daughter, Teresa, who is a mestiza of African descent as well, is portrayed as oblivious of her African lineage. They are ideologically whitened. She appears as happily Americanized, going shopping, eating waffles and talking about North American movie stars (22-23, 25). *La muerte* suggest that post-revolution corruption in Mexico is tied to miscegenation and that *mestizaje,* of the type embodied by Cruz and his lineage, had a negative effect on the Mexican Revolution (50).

In conclusion, *La muerte* is a text where the modern Mexican nation is still being narrated in accordance to the "cosmic race" creed; a belief that the "improvement" of the nation rested on the cleansing, by mixing out, of all black African traces of the population. The novel perpetuates the myth of whitening that underlines the ideology of *mestizaje* in Mexico, as in other parts of the Americas. *La muerte* contributes to the erasure of the path that leads to the African family tree, of Mexican *mestizaje.* Just as *La raza cósmica, El perfil,* and "Los hijos," among other pillars of the imagined modern Mexican nation, *La muerte* reproduces and reinforces the confusion of the origins of the Mexican *mestizo* and his culture: *"a río revuelto ganancia de pescadores."*

La muerte forges and perpetuates stereotypes of black people and their daughters and sons. It thereby codifies them as exhibited under Snead's perspective. The novel marks blacks, mythifies whites and omits mentioning, under a just light, Mexicans of African lineage who do not desire to be whitened and are not servile, tame, submissive, or backward. This renders the African Mexican ahistorical. Just as other Latin American writings studied by Jackson, *La muerte* replaces the historical image of prominent African Mexicans with caricatures.

Notes

[1] This work subscribes to the position that races and all of its nomenclatures are negative social constructs. Also, that racism, a direct negative consequence of such social constructs, and the damages it inflicts on people, are real. This work stands on the premise that all humans are equal and concurrently recognizes that racial terminology is heavily charged and promotes racism. Therefore, it must be emphasized that such language is used here subversively while alternatives are under construction. The aim is to help build a bridge out of Eurocentrism with the very stones that construct it.

[2] The myth of "La Malinche" is found in *Doña Marina* (1833) an historical novel by Ireneo Paz, Octavio Paz' grandfather.

[3] PRI is the acronym for the *Partido Revolucionario Institucional* (Revolutionary Institutional Party) that usurped power immediately after the armed phase of the Mexican Revolution in 1920 and kept direct control of the country until November 2000.

[4] In my essay, "The Afro Dimension of Mexican Carnival: Resisting the Rhetorical Labyrinth of the Discourse on Nation," to be published by Ian I. Smart, I explain the Mexican Mestizo festive spirit in the light of his African heritage.

[5] This type of marriage is described in Celestino Gorostiza's 1952 drama, *El color de nuestra piel* (*The Color of our Skin*). See bibliography.

Conclusion

The Afro element, or black African heritage of Mexican *mestizaje* was erased from memory during the first decades of the twentieth century as the modern nation was being born. The *criollo* government that called itself "revolutionary" launched a mass media campaign to Hispanicize the multicultural, multiethnic, and multilingual population. Education, the arts, and more traditional channels of persuasion, such as radio and newspapers, among others, were recruited and paid for by the government. During this campaign, the Indian heritage started to be extolled, though only as something from the past, along with a supposed Spanish chivalry and love for wisdom and civilization, among other virtues. The Afro characteristics were eradicated from the ideal image of the Mexican mestizo, or "cosmic man," simply by not mentioning them.

Since about the third decade of the sixteenth century, Spanish became the language of the land. All business and governmental activities were conducted in Spanish, although those who spoke and wrote it well were few even among Spaniards. Nevertheless, during the colonial period, Spaniards, through their European imported institutions (clergy, police, army, prisons, among others) persuaded the majority of the Mexican population of a supposed Spanish supremacy. Catholicism became a synonym for honesty and divine truth; European (particularly Spaniard) for civilization and justice; and whiteness for beauty and purity.

To believe in what the invaders thought and taught, at least publicly, became a matter of survival. Of course, believing in itself was not enough to be free from color-of-skin prejudices and social and economic distinctions. Social mobility was nearly impossible to achieve for the daughters and sons of Indians and blacks and their mixes, or the offspring of any of these with the Spaniards. The said offspring were generally bastards. For that matter, not even the legal white children of Spaniards born outside Spain could aspire to positions of control.

Immediately after the wars of independence (1810-1821), the majority of people in Mexico were, just as today, non-whites. The largest minority were the various nations of Amerindians. The second was formed by the *mezclas* (the children of the many mixes that had taken place among Indians, blacks, and Spaniards). Father José María Morelos y Pavón, who became the Independence movement leader upon Father Hidalgo's death, was a mulatto *pardo,* as were an unknown number of *chinaco,* or *mezcla* troops who formed an important part of his army. A similar case was that of General Vicente *el negro* Guerrero who became president for a year before being assassinated right after independence from Spain had been won.

General Guerrero, through the power obtained by the people, officially abolished slavery in 1829. Following his predecessor's (Morelos) desires, it was mandated that racial distinctions should no longer be made in official transactions or documents. These freedom fighters believed that this action would bring equality. By the stroke of the pen, the traces of the Afro heritage of mestizos started to vanish, literally, from what today are valuable historical sources such as Church archives. The stigma of being the descendants of slaves weighed heavily on the population at large. After all, if one was infamous by suspicion of having black blood, it is not be surprising that the population at large soon learned to deny any ties to blackness, even if it was obvious.

When the *criollos* usurped control after the Revolution of 1910-1920, the idea that mestizos were the exclusive offspring of Indians and Spaniards was ripe in the minds of the haves and have-nots alike. Those who advocated the ideology of *mestizaje* saw it as the route to unite a deeply divided nation. Those with black blood saw it as an opportunity to "cleanse" themselves. It was a matter of somehow educating, or persuading everyone to believe in the supremacy of *criollo* culture and that through *mestizaje* or whitening anyone could aspire to upward mobility and thus gain entrance into the "civilized" world.

In 1921, José Vasconcelos enters the picture as Minister of Education and begins transmitting his cosmic race myth through all possible media and thereby whitening the *mezclas* to the level of mestizos by another stroke of the pen. There is no history to be found of *mezcla* resistance to being called the offspring of Indian and Spaniard only. Moreover, there is documentation of the opposite. Aguirre Beltrán (267-92) points out that many a *mezcla* wanted to pass more as Spanish than Indian.

What is interesting is the manner in which the elite, until recently, utilized literature, cinematography, and popular culture among other cultural texts to seize and ensure their stay in power. Through these media channels, the modern nation was narrated and the audiences became persuaded, with the help of self-deceit, that something that never was is. After all, having full control of the media and a strong influence on the canons insured that whatever was said was seldom against the *criollo*-controlled PRI, and the PRI safeguarded those who supported it.

The major problem found in the "cosmic race" revolutionary policy is that what was disseminated about non-white people, particularly the darker people, actually introduced, reproduced, and massively perpetuated stereotypes. It turned the members of a mainly dark population against one another, made a whole country and its people ashamed of their African heritage and propagated the whitening mentality that infects a considerable portion of Mexican mestizos up to the present. Moreover, the said stereotypes, when repeated, reinforce other subjacent symbols, thereby developing codes about visibly black Mexican mestizo-people based more on myth than reality.

As much as this may be argued as a thing of the past, the fact remains that the message contained in the works studied here, in other works mentioned, as well as in many more works all over the Americas, continues to be taught without any warning of their negative effects as far as blacks are concerned. There have been recent classes on the works of well known racists such as Domingo Fausto Sarmiento, José Henriquez Ureña and José Vasconcelos, to mention a few, taught totally ignoring the Modern Languages Association directives about exposing the antihumanist and unscientific character of "lingering racist ideas and materials."

In 1968, immediately before the Olympic games, when the government under Gustavo Diaz Ordaz massacred an "unknown" number of student demonstrators in Tlatelolco, the country, in the words of Ilan Stavans, underwent a deep identity crisis (36). From that day on, institutions began to be scrutinized deeply. The so-called revolutionary government had overstayed its welcome. For its new members, as well as for the people at large, the PRI had become a dinosaur. Mexicans began to search for their identity anew.

Bibliography

Africana. Kwame Anthony Appiah and Henry Louis Gates, Jr., eds. New York: Basic Civitas Books, 1999.

Aggor, Komla F. "Racial Prejudice, Racial Shame: Reading Francisco Arriví's *Máscara puertorriqueña.*" *Bulletin of Hispanic Studies* (1997): 501-12.

Aguirre Bellver, Joaquín. *El borrador de Lazarillo: Texto íntegro.* Madrid: Jaguibel, 1994.

Aguirre Beltrán, Gonzalo. *La población negra de México. Estudio etnohistórico.* México, D.F.: Fondo, 1972 (1a ed. 1946).

Alén Rodríguez, Olavo. *From Afrocuban Music to Salsa.* Book and CD. Berlin: [Pi'ra:na] Musik Produktion & Verlag AG, 1998.

Althoff, Francis Daniel, Jr. "The Afro Hispanic Speech of the Municipio of Cuajinicuilapa, Guerrero." Diss. U of Florida, 1998.

"Americas' 'Oldest' Human Fossil Unveiled." *The Vancouver Sun.* 21 September 1999: A 4c.

Andrade, Arnulfo. "La danza popular mexicana: Nayarit." *Instituto Cultural Raíces Mexicanas.* 6 October 1999 <http://www.folklorico.com/folk-dances/nayarit/mestizo-nayarit.html>.

Angelitos Negros. Dir. Joselito Rodríguez. Perf. Pedro Infante, Emilia Guiú, Rita Montaner. Estudios Tepeyac, 1948.

Assunção, Fernando O. *El tango y sus circunstancias* (1880-1920). Buenos Aires: El Ateneo, 1984.

Atlas cultural de México: Lingüística. México, D. F.: Planeta, 1988.

Bar-Lewaw, Itzhak. *Introducción crítico-biográfica a José Vasconcelos (1882-1959).* Madrid: Ediciones Latinoamericanas, 1965.

Bartolomé, Miguel Alberto. *Gente de costumbre y gente de razón: Las identidades étnicas de México.* México D.F.: Siglo Veintiuno, 1997.

Basañez Arana, Margarita, and Ricardo Valdés Ruvalcava, eds. *Distrito Federal: Monografía estatal.* México, D. F.: SEP, 1992.

Basave Benítez, Agustín. *México mestizo: Análisis del nacionalismo mexicano en torno a la mestizofilia de Andrés Molina Enriquez.* México, D.F.: Fondo de Cultura, 1992.

Bennett, Herman Lee. "Lovers Family and Friends: The Formation of Afro-Mexico, 1580-1810." Diss. Duke U, 1993.

Brushwood, John S. *Mexico in its Novel: A Nation's Search for Identity*. Austin: U of Texas P, 1966.

Bueno, Salvador. "El negro en *El Periquillo Sarniento*: antirracismo de Lizardi". *Cuadernos Americanos* CLXXXIII, 4 (1972): 124-39.

Carraher, Janice. "La Bamba Explained: Or the Music of Veracruz." *Mexico Connect*. 6 October 1999 <http://www.mexconnect.com/mex_/travel/jcar/jcbamba.html>.

Carroll, Patrick J. "Los mexicanos negros, el mestizaje y los fundamentos olvidados de la 'Raza Cósmica': una perspectiva regional". *Historia Mexicana* 44 (January-March 1995): 403-38.

Castro Gómez, Santiago. "Imaginarios sociales y estética de lo bello en el modernismo hispanoamericano." *Crítica de la razón latinoamericana*. Barcelona: Puvill, 1996.

Cepeda, William, dir. *Grupo Afro-Boricua from Puerto Rico*. CD Recording. Huntington: Blue Jackel Entertainment, 1998.

Clark, Jonathan D. "Entry on the Word Mariachi from *The Latino Encyclopedia*." *A Brief History of the Mariachi Tradition*. October 6, 1999 <http://www.mariach-publishing.com/MER/entry_on_the_word_mariachi.htm>.

Cord, William O. trans. *The Futile Life of Pito Pérez*. New Jersey: Prentice Hall, 1966. (Original novel by José Rubén Romero published in 1938 under the title *La vida inútil de Pito Pérez*).

Crow, John A. *Spain: The Root and the Flower*. Berkeley: U of California P, *1985* (1st ed. 1963).

Davis, James F. *Who is Black? One Nation's Definition*. University Park: The Pennsylvania State U P, 1998 (1st ed. 1991).

Díaz y de Ovando, Clementina. "Introducción." *Antología de Vicente Riva Palacio*. México, D.F.: UNAM, 1976.

Duncan, Cynthia. "Language as a Barrier to Communication Between the Classes in Rosario Castellanos's 'La tregua' and José Revueltas's 'El lenguaje de nadie.'" *Hispania* 74 (December 1991): 868-75.

Duncan, Quince. "Racismo: Apuntes para una teoría general del racismo". *Cultura negra y teología*. San José: Dei, 1986.

Esteva-Fabregat, Claudio. *Mestizaje in Ibero-America*. Trans. John Wheat. Tucson: The U of Arizona P, 1995 (Original 1987).

Fanon, Frantz. *Black Skin, White Masks*. Trans. Charles Lam Markmann. New York: Grove Press, 1967. Originally published in French in 1952.

Fernández de Lizardi, José Joaquín. *El Periquillo Sarniento*. Madrid: Ediciones Cátedra, 1997 (1ª ed. 1816).

Fischer, Lucy, ed. *Imitation of Life*. Rutgers Films in Print. New Brunswick: Rutgers UP, 1991.

Florescano, Enrique. "La interpretación del siglo XIX". *Cincuenta años de historia en México: En el cincuentenario del Centro de Estudios Históricos*. México D. F.: El Colegio de México, 1991.

Friedemann, Nina S de. "Negros en Colombia: Identidad e invisibilidad". *Hacia nuevos modelos de relaciones interculturales*. Comp.Guillermo Bonfil Batalla. México: Consejo Nacional Para la Cultura y las Artes, 1993.

Fuentes, Carlos. *La muerte de Artemio Cruz*. México: Fondo, 1990. (13a impresión).

Galeano, Eduardo. *Las venas abiertas de América Latina*. México: Siglo XXI, 1988. (3a ed.).

García de León, Antonio. "Contrapunto barroco en el Veracruz colonial". *Modernidad, mestizaje cultural, ethos barroco*. México, D. F.: UNAM y El Equilibrista, 1994.

García Riera, Emilio. *México visto por el cine extranjero*. Vol. 3. México, D.F.: Era, 1988.

Garrido, Felipe, ed. *Lecciones de Historia de México*. 2 vols. México, D.F.: Secretaría de Educación Pública, 1994.

Gómez Izquierdo, José Jorge. *El movimiento antichino en México (1871-1934)*. 2 México, D.F: Instituto Nacional de Antropología e Historia, 1991.

González Casanova, Pablo. *La literatura perseguida en la crisis de la Colonia*. México, D.F.: El Colegio de México, 1958.

González El-Hilali, Anita. "Performing Mestizaje: Official Culture and Identity in Veracruz, Mexico." Diss. U of Wisconsin, 1997.

González Navarro, Moisés. *Los extranjeros en México y los mexicanos en el extranjero (1821-1970)*. 3 vols. México, D. F.: El Colegio de México, 1994.

Gorostiza, Celestino. *El color de nuestra piel*. New York: MacMillan, 1966.

Grimes, Barbara, ed. "Mexico" *Ethnologue*. Junio 8, 1999 <http://www.sil.org/ethnologue/Countries/Mexi.html>.

Güemes, César. "Contar la otra versión de la novela: Carlos Fuentes.*" La Jornada Online*. 16 March 2000 <http://www.jornada.unam.mx/1999/mar99/990313/cul-fuentes.html>.

Guzmán, Martín Luis. *Obras Completas*. 2 volúmenes. México, D. F.: Compañía General de Ediciones, 1961.

106

Gyurko, Lanin A. "Structure and Theme in Fuentes' *La muerte de Artemio Cruz*". *Symposium* 34, (1980): 29-41.

Harris, Joseph E. The African Diaspora Map—1. *Conexoes* 3. (1 May 1991): 8-9.

Historia General de México: versión 2000. Preparada por El Centro de Estudios Históricos. México, D.F.: El Colegio de México, 2000.

INEGI. Instituto Nacional de Estadística, Geografía e Informática. 10 August 2000 <http://www.inegi.gob.mx/>.

Jackson, Richard L. *The Black Image in Latin American Literature*. Albuquerque: U of New Mexico, 1976.

_____. "Black Phobia and the White Aesthetic in Spanish American Literature." *Hispania* 58 (1975): 467-80.

_____. *Black Writers in Latin America*. Albuquerque: U of New Mexico P, 1979.

Kattan-Ibarra, Juan. *Perspectivas culturales de Hispanoamérica*. Lincolnwood: NTC Publishing, Co., 1990.

Kiple, Kenneth F., and Kriemhild Conee Ornelas, eds. *The Cambridge World History of Food*. 2 vols. Cambridge: Cambridge UP, 2000.

Knight, Alan. "Racism, Revolution and Indigenismo: México 1910-1940." *The Idea of Race in Latin America, 1870-1940*. Ed. Richard Graham. Austin: U of Texas, 1990.

Kutzinski, Vera M. "Afro-Hispanic American Literature." *The Cambridge History of Latin American Literature*. Vol. 2: The Twentieth Century. Eds. Roberto González Echevarría & Enrique Pupo Walker. Cambridge: Cambridge UP. (1996): 164-194.

Lewis, Marvin A. *Afro-Argentinian Discourse: Another Dimension of the Black Diaspora*. Columbia: U of Missouri P, 1996.

Mandela, Nelson. *Habla Mandela*. New York: Pathfinder, 1986.

Martínez Montiel, Luz María. "Mexico's Third Root." *Africa's Legacy in Mexico*. 2 August 1999 <http://educate.si.edu/migrations/legacy/almthird.html>.

_____. *Negros en América*. México, D.F.: Mapfre, 1992.

Maza, Maximiliano. "Más de cien años del cine mexicano". 15 July 1999 <http://www.mty.itsm.mx/dcic/carreras/lcc/cine_mex/frorr>.

McCaa, Robert. "The Peopling of Mexico from Origins to Revolution." 15 July 1999 <rmccaa@tc.umn.edu>.

Melgoza Paralizábal, Arturo. *El maravilloso monstruo alado*. México: UNAM, 1996.

Merriam-Webster Collegiate Dictionary. 10th ed. 1995.

Monsiváis, Carlos. "Las mitologías del cine mexicano". 28 November 2000 <http:www.cinemateca.org.ve/visual-textos.htm>.

_____. "Notas sobre la cultura mexicana en el siglo XX". *Historia General de México 2*. México, D. F.: El Colegio de México, 1988.

Mr. Rock 'n' Roll: The Allan Freed Story. (1999 drama). BCTV Sun 17 October (1999): 9:00 p.m.

Mullen, Edward J. *Afro-Cuban Literature: Critical Junctures*. Westport: Greenwood, 1998.

Muñoz Batista, Jorge. "Samuel Ramos y la educación mexicana". Universidad La Salle. 8 August 2000 <http://hemerodigital.unam.mx/ANUIES/lasalle /logos/75/sec_6.htm>.

Museos de México Online. UNAM Servicios Hemerográficos: Mérida. 30 September 1999.

La Nación <http://www.nacion.co.cr/ln_ee/ESPECIALES/ raices/preafric.html>. San José, Costa Rica. 6 October 1999.

Nascimento, Abdias do. *O genocidio do negro brasileiro: processo de um racismo mascarado*. Rio de Janeiro: Paz e Terra, 1978.

Neglia, Herminio G. *El hecho teatral en Hispanoamérica*. Roma: Bulzoni, 1985.

La Negra Angustias. Dir. Matilde Landeta. Perf. María Elena Marqués, Agustín Isunza, Eduardo Arozamena, Gilberto González, et al. Estudios Churubusco, 1949.

Niño, Hugo. "El etnotexto: voz y actuación la oralidad". *Revista de crítica latinoamericana* 47 (1998): 109-21.

Ochoa Serrano, Álvaro. *Afrodescendientes: Sobre piel canela*. Zamora: El Colegio de Michoacán, 1997.

Ortega, Julio. "Diez novelas del XX". *La Jornada Semanal*, 24 de enero de 1999. Online 16 March 2000.

Palmer, Colin A. "A Legacy of Slavery". *Africa's Legacy in Mexico*. 2 August 1999 <http://educate.si.edu/migrations/ legacy/almleg.html>.

Payno, Manuel. *Crónicas de Viaje: Por Veracruz y otros lugares*. Obras Completas I. Boris Rosen Jélomer compiler. México, D.F.: Consejo Nacional para la Cultura y las Artes, 1996.

Paz, Octavio. "Los hijos de la Malinche". *El Laberinto de la soledad*. México: Fondo, 1989 (18th ed.).

Pei, Mario, and Frank Gaynor. *A Dictionary of Linguistics*. New York: Philosophical Library, 1954.

108

Pequeño Larousse Ilustrado. Ramón García-Pelayo y Gross, ed. México D.F.: Larousse, 1989.

Pérez Fernández, Rolando Antonio. "El verbo chingar una palabra clave". *El rostro colectivo de la nación mexicana*. Morelia: Instituto de Investigaciones Históricas de la Universidad Michoacana de San Nicolás de Hidalgo (1997): 305-24.

Pérez Monfort, Ricardo. *Estampas de nacionalismo popular mexicano: Ensayos sobre cultura popular y nacionalismo*. México D.F.: CIESA, 1994.

Perú, Música Negra: El Negro Maravilla, cajonero y taxista, de La Victoria a Lima. France: A.S.P.I.C., 1992.

Peruvian Cuisine Online. 8 August 2000 <http://www.Perutrvel2000.com/recipes1htm>.

Piedra, José. "Literary Whiteness and the Afro-Hispanic Difference." New *Literary History: A Journal of Theory and Interpretation* 18, No. 2 (1987): 303-32.

Prieto Hernández, Ana María. *Acerca de la pendenciera e indisciplinada vida de los léperos capitalinos*. México, D.F.: CONACULTA, 2001.

Ramérez Pimienta, Juan Carlos. "Del rancho al arrabal: guías para ayudar a formar un estado-nación en el cine mexicano de la Época de oro". *Nuevo Texto crítico* 19/20 (1997): 211-21.

Ramírez Cuevas, Jesús. "Queremos la autonomía para evitar que el país termine hecho añicos y malbaratado: Marcos". *La Jornada Online*. 27 February 2001 <http://www.jornada.unam.mx/2001/feb01/010227/009nlpol.html>.

Ramos, Samuel. *El perfil del hombre y la cultura en México*. México, D.F.: UNAM, 1963 (1ª ed. 1934).

Rejano, Juan. *La esfinge mestiza*. Madrid: Cupsa, 1978.

Revueltas, José. *Cuestionamientos e intenciones*. Presentación, recopilación y notas de Andrea Revueltas y Philippe Cheron. México D. F.: Era, 1978.

Reynoso Medina, Araceli. "Esclavos y condenados: Trabajo y etnicidad en el obraje de Posadas". *El rostro colectivo de la nación mexicana*. Morelia: Instituto de Investigaciones Históricas de la Universidad Michoacana de San Nicolás de Hidalgo, (1997): 17-35.

Riding, Alan. *Distant Neighbors: A portrait of the Mexicans*. New York: Vintage, 1989 (1st ed. 1984).

Riva Palacio, Vicente. *Calvario y Tabor*. México D.F.: Porrúa, 2000. (1st ed. 1868).

109

Rodríguez, Santiago. "Hispanics in the United States: An Insight Into Group Characteristics." 30 September 1999 <http://www .harcourtcollege.com/marketing/students/consumer.htm>.

Romero, José Rubén. *La vida inútil de Pito Pérez*. México, D, F.: Porrúa, 1995 (1st ed. 1938).

Rowe, William, and Vivian Schelling. *Memory and Modernity: Popular Culture in Latin America*. London: Verso, 1996.

Said, Edward W. *Culture and Imperialism*. New York: Vintage, 1994.

Sepúlveda, María Teresa. *Magia, brujería y supersticiones en México*. México, D. F.: Everest, 1983.

Sevilla, Paco. "Flamenco: The Early Years." *John's Flamenco Online*. 6 October 1999 <ftp://ftp.std.com/ftp/nonprofits/dance/ Flamenco/flamenco-history-1of2txt>.

Shohat, Ella, and Robert Stam. *Unthinking Eurocentrism: Multiculturalism and the Media*. London: Routledge, 1994.

Simon Wiesenthal Center Multimedia Learning Center Online. 1 November 1999 <http://motlc.wiesenthal.org/pages/t026/ t02612.html>.

Snead, James. *White Screens Black Images: Hollywood from the dark side*. Eds. Colin MacCabe & Cornel West. London: Routledge, 1994.

Sommer, Doris. "Irresistible Romance: The Foundational Fictions of Latin America." *Nation and Narration*. Ed. Homi K. Bhabha. London: Routledge, 1990.

Stavans, Ilan. *The Riddle of Cantinflas: Essays on Hispanic Popular Culture*. Albuquerque: U of New Mexico P, 1999.

Thomas, Hugh. *Cuba or the Pursuit of Freedom*. New York: Da Capo, 1998 (1st ed. 1971).

Tolstoy, Count Lev N. *War and Peace* vol. III-IV. Trans. Leo Weiner. Boston: Dana Estes & Co.,1904.

Truque Vélez, Colombia. "Louvabagu (el otro lado lejano) o un teatro latinoamericano de la identidad: entrevista realizada por Colombia Vélez a Rafael Murillo-Selva Rendón". *Afro-Hispanic Review* Vol. 18, n. 1 (Spring 1999): 34-7.

Van Sertima, Ivan. *They Came Before Columbus*. New York: Random, 1976.

Vargas Martínez, Ubaldo. *Morelos: Siervo de la nación*. México.D.F.: Porrúa, 1966.

Vasconcelos, José. *La raza cósmica: misión de la raza iberoamericana*. Madrid: Agencia Mundial de Librerías, 1925.

Vaughn, Bobby. *"The Black Mexico Homepage" Online*. 2 July1999 <http://www.stanford.edu/~bvaughn/>.

Vincent, Ted. "Racial Amnesia-African Puerto Rico and México." *Ishmael Reed's Konch Magazine Online*. 16 July 1999 <http://www.ishmaelreedpub.com/vincent.html>.

"¡Viva México! : En septiembre vive la alegría de la tradición y pinta con nuestros colores tu corazón". Anuncio publicitario de la compañía Herdez (un corazón tricolor evocando la bandera mexicana, en su centro en donde va el color blanco la foto de un bebé de ojos verdeazules). *Reforma*. 15 September (1998): E10.

Voices and Visions. Langston Hughes. Direction: St. Clair Bourne. Production: The New York Center for the Visual Arts, 1995.

Walker, Thomas. "Hendrix in Black and White." *The Vancouver Sun*. 18 September (1999): A21.

Webster's New Collegiate Dictionary. 1956.

Wilson, Rita. "Pedro Infante Movies: 1948-1949." *Online*. February 5, 2000 <rlwls@alumni.si.umich.edu>.

Wilt, David. Unpublished information requested and received on February 17, 2000. <dw45@umail.umd.e>.

Zaire. *Ethnologue: Areas: Africa Online*. 30 September 1999 <http://www.sil.org/ethnologue/countries/Zair.html>.

Zapata Olivella, Manuel. "Omnipresencia Africana en la Civilización Universal". *PALARA* 4 (2000):5-15.

Zúñiga, Víctor. "Los 'otros' mexicanos ('indios' y 'pochos'): la cuestión de la diferencia en México". *El Debate Nacional: IV Nuevos actores sociales*. Esthela Gutiérrez Garza, *et al* coordinadores. México D.F.: Diana, 1997.

About the Author

Dr. Marco Polo Hernández Cuevas is an Assistant Professor of Spanish Language & Literature at Emporia State University in Kansas, USA. He holds a Ph.D. in Hispanic Studies from the University of British Columbia, Vancouver, Canada; a Master of Arts in Spanish Language and Literature from Portland State University, Portland, Oregon, USA; and a B.A. in General Studies and Spanish Language and Literature from Portland State University as well. The *Afro-Hispanic Review* and *PALARA* have published various academic essays by him where he exhibits the Africaness of Mexicaness. He has made presentations at world-renowned schools such as the *Escuela Nacional de Antropología e Historia* (National School of Anthropology and History) (2002) in Mexico City, Mexico; The University of British Columbia, Canada (1999); and *Universidad Nacional Autónoma de México* (National University of Mexico) (1992) among others. Presently he is working with Carnival in Mexico and its ties to the rest of the Americas and the African Mexicans and the XIX century novel.

Index

114

116